P9-DBV-114

the VERBAL MATH LESSON

Step-by-Step Math
without
Pencil or Paper

1
LEVEL

Michael Levin M.D.
Charan Langton M.S.

MOUNTCASTLE COMPANY

MAR 16 2009 ROC
872.72
L665v

The

VERBAL
MATH LESSON

LEVEL 1

Michael Levin M.D.
Charan Langton M.S.

Copyright 2008 Mountcastle Company
First Edition May 2008

Edited by Ashley Kuhre
Design by Pegin S. McDermott

Manufactured in the United States of America

Cover Photo from BigStockPhotos

ISBN 978-0-913063-09-5
Library of Congress Control Number: 2007938785

*All Rights Reserved. No part of this book may be reproduced or utilized in any form
or by any means, electronic passages, posting, mechanical including photocopying
and recording on any storage device and retrieval system without the written per-
mission of the publisher.*

Mountcastle Company
Contact: mntcastle@earthlink.net
www.mathlesson.com

Just a little everyday;
        That's the way
Children learn to read and write,
Bit by bit and mite by mite,
        Never anyone, I say,
Leaps to knowledge and its power
Slowly, slowly - hour by hour-
        That's the way;
        Just a little everyday.
                        - Ella Wheeler Wilcox

The Lessons

Introduction

This course is designed to make math fun for your young child. As in learning to read, where children need to develop a basic vocabulary for fluency, the verbal problems in this course also build a basic mathematical vocabulary that your child needs to progress further. Similar to our step-by-step reading program, the Reading Lesson, the Verbal Math Lesson strengthens the ability to do math quickly.

Written math makes simple arithmetic tedious for young children, particularly for those who don't like to write. Often, an insistence on worksheets that require more writing effort than math leads to a dislike for math in general. We want your child to like math, and learning math as a game helps this process.

This book is intended for children in grades K-1. The problems must be read to the child, so all calculations are done mentally and without the use of pencil or paper.

How accurate and speedy should your child be? The answer is difficult to give. The human brain, particularly a child's brain, is not an accurate machine and memory is not perfect. Children differ in their ability to develop accurate and speedy recall. A general guideline of four seconds can be used for most problems as a gauge of skill.

Your child should be able to do the majority of these problems correctly the first time. If not, repeat the lesson the next day. Before you progress to a new lesson, make sure that your child can do most of the problems in the current lesson easily and quickly.

Most children can easily do 20 to 30 problems a day but short periods of practice are better in developing skill and maintaining interest. Repeat each lesson until the child gets nearly all the problems correct.

The best way to do these problems is to read the problem to the child and wait for the answer. If your child has difficulty understanding the problem, you may re-read the problem one or more times until it is well understood.

You can either read the explanations in the beginning of the lessons aloud or read them to yourself and then explain the concepts in your own words.

Subordinate speed to accuracy, but do not neglect speed. Ability to answer these simple problems quickly means mastery. Excessive time on each problem tells you that the child is not ready to move on and that the lesson might need to be repeated.

Be creative! Compose problems yourself along the theme of the lesson using fuuny episodes from your daily life. Ask your child to make his or her own problems for you to solve.

Who's ready for this course?

Most children are able to understand mathematical concepts long before they are ready to read. You can start this course at any age, if your child is able to do the following.

• Is able to count up to 100. (Occasional errors are acceptable.)

• Can dentify written numbers. (Single and double-digits)

• Understands the concepts of "same as", "more than" and "less than" when referring to numbers and quantities.

• Knows the difference between right and left and, hopefully, between right and wrong. Although not a primary object of Verbal Math Lesson, the course tries to present the problems with regard to basic societal values and parental authority.

• Recognizes basic shapes. (Circle, triangle, square, diamond and star)

• Has a basic, conceptual understanding of measurements of length (inches and feet) and weight (ounces, pounds, tons).

We are pleased to bring you this new concept of teaching math and would be happy to hear of your experiences with it. Please contact us with suggestions and corrections.

Best wishes,

Michael Levin
Charan Langton
www.mathlesson.com

Working with Nothing
Let's learn the concept of 0.

Teacher: Clear a desk or a table. Place a pen and say: "There is one pen on the table." Ask: "Are there any pencils on the table?" The answer should be: NO.

Say: "There is one pen and no pencils on the table. In math we say, there is one pen and zero pencils on the table. Zero means nothing."

Exercise I

1. If my feet are bare, that means I am wearing zero socks.

2. If the road is empty, that means there are zero cars on the road.

3. The garage was empty. Until my mom parked her car in it, there were zero cars in the garage.

4. If no one puts money in a piggy bank, it has zero money.

5. Before I planted a rose in an empty garden, there were zero roses growing there.

6. After I took the last cookie from the jar, there were zero cookies left in the jar.

7. Ask your child to make examples of zero.

Exercise II

⇨ *The rule: If you add a zero to a number, the number does not change.*

$1 + 0 = 1$ $2 + 0 = 2$ $3 + 0 = 3$ $10 + 0 = 10$

⇨ *The rule: If you add a number to a zero, the number does not change.*
It stays the same.

$0 + 1 = 1$ $0 + 2 = 2$ $0 + 5 = 5$ $0 + 9 = 9$

Exercise III

1. We had 2 pictures on the wall and put no new pictures up. How many pictures are on the wall? *Ans:* 2 pictures

    Solution: 2 pictures + 0 pictures = 2 pictures. So, the answer is 2 pictures.

2. A pet store had 4 birds in a cage. No new birds were put in the cage. How many birds are in the cage now? *Ans:* 4 birds.

3. There were 10 monkeys on a tree. No new monkeys came. How many monkeys are on the tree now? *Ans:* 10 monkeys.

4. The table was empty before I put 4 plates on it. How many plates are on the table now? *Ans:* 4 plates.

    Solution: mathematically speaking, 0 plates + 4 plates = 4 plates. Therefore, the answer is 4 plates.

5. On an empty field. The construction crew built 5 houses on a field. How many houses are on the field now? *Ans:* 5 houses $(0 + 5 = 5)$.

6. My backyard had no holes. Then 3 gophers dug 6 holes. How many holes are in my backyard now? *Ans:* 6 holes.

    Solution: Don't confuse holes with 3 gophers. There could have been hundreds of hole-digging gophers, but we are not counting the gophers, only the holes they dug.

7. The page was empty. Then 2 children drew 3 squares in 4 minutes. How many squares are on the page now? *Ans:* 3 squares, because $(0 + 3 = 3)$.

Counting and simple adding

Exercise I

Count up to 5 forwards and then backwards.
Count forwards and backwards from 4 to 10.
Count backwards from 13.
Count backwards from 16 to 10.
Count backwards from 20 to 15.
Count forwards from 20 to 30.
Count from 30 to 45, forwards and backwards.
Count forward from 1 to 9, skipping every other number:
  1, skip 2, 3, skip 4, 5, skip 6, 7, skip 8, 9.
  Instead of skipping, child may whisper the number.
Now, count from 2 to 10 skipping every other number:
  2, skip 3, 4, skip 5, 6, skip 7, 8, skip 9, 10.
What comes after 2? 5? 7? 8? 10?
What comes after 11? 13? 14? 16? 19?
What comes after 22? 25? 31? 33? 37?
What comes before 46? 49? 52? 75? 91?
What comes before 21? 31? 41? 51? 53?
What comes before 20? 30? 40? 50? 60?
What comes before and after 33? 22? 67?

Exercise II

I'll give you two numbers; tell me which one comes first when counting.

7 or 5	*Ans:* 5
8 or 7	*Ans:* 7
13 or 15	*Ans:* 13
9 or 11	*Ans:* 9
28 or 41	*Ans:* 28
17 or 13	*Ans:* 13
54 or 45	*Ans:* 45
23 or 32	*Ans:* 23
87 or 78	*Ans:* 78
99 or 88	*Ans:* 88

Now, I'll give you 3 numbers, can you place them in order from the smallest to the largest?

6, 8, and 7	*Ans:* 6, 7, 8
9, 4, and 6	*Ans:* 4, 6, 9
6, 2, and 4	*Ans:* 2, 4, 6
8, 3, and 5	*Ans:* 3, 5, 8
4, 0, and 3	*Ans:* 0, 3, 4
8, 5, and 7	*Ans:* 5, 7, 8
10, 9, and 7	*Ans:* 7, 9, 10

Exercise III

Count forward from 1 to 20, skipping every 2 numbers:
1, (skip 2 and 3), 4, (skip 5 and 6), 7, (skip 8 and 9), etc.
Instead of skipping, child may whisper the number.

You might want to make your own skipping numbers exercises. Instead of skipping you can also take turns in counting.
For example: You say: 1. The child says: 2, 3.
You say: 4. The child says: 5, 6. Etc.

Now, count from 2 to 20 skipping every 2 numbers:
2, (skip 3 and 4), 5, (skip 6 and 7), 8, (skip 9 and 10), etc.

Word Problems

1. If I have 2 cookies and I get 1 more, how many cookies do I have?
    Ans: 3 cookies.

2. There is 1 sparrow and 2 black birds sitting in the tree. How many birds
    are sitting in the tree? *Ans:* 3 birds.

3. First I saw a white car go by, then a red car and then a white car. How
    many cars did I see? *Ans:* 3 cars.

4. I have 2 best friends. Then I made 1 more best friend. How many best
    friends do I have? *Ans:* 3 best friends.

5. I was counting and forgot what comes after 12. Can you tell me what
    number I forgot? *Ans:* 13.

6. In the red box there are 6 marbles and in the blue box there are 9 marbles.
    Which box has more marbles? *Ans:* Blue box.

7. One team has 6 kids and the other team has 5 kids. Which team has fewer
    kids? *Ans:* The team with 5 kids.

8. I am counting by skipping one number. I say 7, what number will I say next? *Ans:* 9.

9. How many numbers are between 1 and 4? *Ans:* 2 numbers; they are 3 and 4.

10. How many numbers are between 1 and 6?
    Ans: 4 numbers; they are 2, 3, 4 and 5.

11. How many numbers are between 3 and 6? *Ans:* 2 numbers; they are 4 and 5.

12. How many numbers are between 4 and 6? *Ans:* 1 number. It is 5.

13. How many numbers are between 5 and 10?
    Ans: 4 numbers; they are 6, 7, 8, and 9.

14. How many numbers are between 1 and 11?
    Ans: 9 numbers. They are 2, 3, 4, 5, 6, 7, 8, 9, and 10.

15. I have three coins in one hand and one coin in the other hand. How many coins am I hiding in both hands? *Ans:* 4 coins.

16. Ann has 2 sisters and 2 brothers. How many brothers and sisters does she have? *Ans:* 4 brothers and sisters.

17. How many children are there in Ann's family? *Ans:* 5 children.

18. Meena was counting and got stuck at 43. What's the next number after 43? *Ans:* 44.

19. Meena got to 53. What number comes before 53? *Ans:* 52.

20. Their team has one more kid than ours. We have 5 kids on our team. How many do they have? *Ans:* 6 kids.

21. An ice cream store sold 11 vanilla cones and 1 chocolate cone. How many ice cream cones did it sell? *Ans:* 12 ice cream cones.

22. Millie knows 33 jokes. Billy knows one less. How many jokes does Billy know? *Ans:* 32 jokes.

23. An archer shot 55 arrows. All but 1 hit the target. How many arrows hit the target? *Ans:* 54 arrows.

24. A soccer team scored 9 goals and then 1 more goal. How many goals did the team score? *Ans:* 10 goals.

25. Mr. Lopez took 1 apple from the basket that had 20 apples in it. How many apples are in the basket now? *Ans:* 19 apples.

26. There were 29 students in the class and then a new student came. How many students are in the class now? *Ans:* 30 students.

27. Michelle lost 16 tennis balls and then lost 1 more. How many tennis balls did she lose? *Ans:* 17 balls.

28. A mom bought 9 T-shirts and then returned 1 T-shirt back to the store. How many shirts did she keep? *Ans:* 8 shirts.

29. An actress had 50 dresses and bought 1 more. How many dresses does she have now? *Ans:* 51 dresses.

30. Oliver had a 12-foot wire and cut off a 1 foot piece. How long is the wire now? *Ans:* 11 feet.

31. Leo has $40 in his wallet and $1 in his pocket. How much money does he have all together? *Ans:* $41.

32. The animal shelter has 47 cats and got 1 more. How many cats do they have now? *Ans:* 48 cats.

33. I was sitting alone and then two of my friends came and sat next to me. How of many of us are sitting together? *Ans:* 3.

34. I have 6 coins and Sheila has 5. Who has fewer coins? *Ans:* Sheila.

35. A park has 37 birch trees and 29 aspen trees. Are there more birches than aspens? *Ans:* Yes.

Addition up to 6

Exercise I

What number comes after 3?   *Ans:* 4
What number comes after 0?   *Ans:* 1
What number comes after 5?   *Ans:* 6
What number comes before 5?   *Ans:* 4
What number comes before 3?   *Ans:* 2
What number comes before 1?   *Ans:* 0

⇨ *The rule of reversibles: When adding numbers, it doesn't matter which number goes first. The answer will be the same.*

Example:
2 + 1 equals 3, and also 1 + 2 is 3   3 + 1 = 4, and also 1 + 3 = 4
1 + 4 = 5, and also 4 + 1 = 5   2 + 3 = 5, and also 3 + 2 = 5

Exercise II

1 + 1 = 2	4 + 1 = 5	2 + 1 = 3	2 + 2 = 4	0 + 2 = 2
1 + 2 = 3	2 + 1 = 3	3 + 1 = 4	4 + 2 = 6	1 + 1 + 1 = 3
1 + 3 = 4	2 + 2 = 4	2 + 3 = 5	2 + 4 = 6	1 + 0 = 1
1 + 4 = 5	3 + 2 = 5	2 + 4 = 6	2 + 3 = 5	1 + 2 + 0 = 3
1 + 5 = 6	1 + 3 = 4	2 + 1 = 3	4 + 0 = 4	1 + 2 + 1 = 4
1 + 2 = 3	2 + 3 = 5	1 + 1 = 2	0 + 3 = 3	0 + 4 = 4
2 + 1 = 3	1 + 2 = 3	3 + 2 = 5	5 + 1 = 6	6 + 0 = 6
1 + 3 = 4	2 + 3 = 5	4 + 1 = 5	0 + 1 = 1	0 + 0 = 0
3 + 1 = 4	3 + 2 = 5	2 + 3 = 5	3 + 3 = 6	1 + 1 + 1 = 3

Exercise III

? + 2 = 3   Say: Which number and 2 together make 3?   *Ans:* 1
Comment: This exercise uses subtraction to solve these problems and may be a bit difficult for a young child.

? + 1 = 3	? + 2 = 4	? + 3 = 5	? + 0 = 6	? + 3 = 6
? + 2 = 3	? + 0 = 4	? + 2 = 5	? + 4 = 6	? + 2 = 6
? + 3 = 3	? + 4 = 4	? + 0 = 5	? + 5 = 6	? + 1 = 1
? + 1 = 4	? + 1 = 2	? + 4 = 5	? + 4 = 6	? + 4 = 6
? + 3 = 4	? + 1 = 5	? + 5 = 5	? + 1 = 6	? + 5 = 5

Word Problems

1. Jack had 2 candies. Jill gave him 1 more. How many does he have now?
    Ans: 3 candies.

2. Jill has 2 cookies and Jack gave her 2 more. How many does she have now? *Ans:* 4 cookies.

3. I have 1 white shirt and 3 red shirts. How many shirts do I have?
    Ans: 4 shirts.

4. There are 3 boys and 1 girl in the room. How many kids are in the room?
    Ans: 4 kids.

5. I had 2 pencils and found 2 more in my desk. How many pencils do I have now? *Ans:* 4 pencils.

6. I have 2 coins in one hand and 2 coins in the other hand. How many coins do I have? *Ans:* 4 coins.

7. Mary's mom told her to pick up 2 apples from the table and 3 more apples from the pantry. How many apples did Mary pick up? *Ans:* 5 apples.

8. Annie put 3 snails on the table. Her brother put 2 more. How many snails are on the table? *Ans:* 5 snails.

9. Alex is 2 years old.
    a) How old she will be in 1 year? *Ans:* 3 years.
    b) In 2 years? *Ans:* 4 years.
    c) In 3 years? *Ans:* 5 years.
    d) In 4 years? *Ans:* 6 years.

10. Nina has 3 brothers. Last month a baby sister was born. How many brothers and sisters does Nina have? *Ans:* 4 brothers and sisters.

11. Britta lives with her mom, dad, and grandmother. She has 2 sisters. How many people live in Britta's house? *Ans:* 6 people.

12. Sam lives with his mom, grandmother and grandfather. He has one brother. How many people live in Sam's house? *Ans:* 5 people.

13. Jill ate 1 plum, 1 apple and 3 cookies. How many different pieces did she eat? *Ans:* 5 pieces.

14. Camilla has 2 red dresses, 2 yellow dresses and 1 green dress. How many dresses does she have? *Ans:* 5 dresses.

15. I had 5 beetles and found one more. How many do I have now?
    Ans: 6 beetles.

16. I put 4 grapes on a plate. Then I added 2 more grapes. How many grapes are on the plate? *Ans:* 6 grapes.

17. I had 3 friends and then 2 more kids became my friends. How many friends do I have now? *Ans:* 5 friends.

18. A car has 2 wheels in front and 2 in the back. How many wheels does the car have? *Ans:* 4 wheels.

19. Our black dog had 3 puppies. Our gray dog had 2 puppies. How many puppies do we have? *Ans:* 5 puppies.

20. How many fingers do you have on your right hand?
    Ans: 5 or 4. Both answers can be considered correct.

21. Yesterday, Mike planted 1 tree and today he planted 3 more. How many trees did he plant? *Ans:* 4 trees.

22. Our car has 4 tires. One spare tire is in the trunk. How many tires does the car have if I count the one in the trunk? *Ans:* 5 tires.

23. Omar and Tricia fed 3 squirrels and also 3 rabbits. How many animals did they feed? *Ans:* 6 animals.

24. Natasha sent 2 postcards to her grandparents, 1 card to her uncle and 1 to her sister. How many cards did she send? *Ans:* 4 cards.

25. A guard helped 3 children across the street and then 3 more. How many children did she help to the other side of the street? *Ans:* 6 children.

26. Our 3 rabbits ate 4 carrots. My neighbor's 2 rabbits ate 2 carrots. How many carrots did all the rabbits eat?
    Ans: 6 carrots. Remember, we are counting the carrots, not the rabbits, no matter how many of them are there.

27. There were 2 parrots in the cage; 2 more parrots were put into it. How many parrots are in the cage now? *Ans:* 4 parrots.

28. A singer recorded 2 songs the day before yesterday, 2 songs yesterday, and 2 today. How many songs did he record altogether?
    Ans: 6 songs.

29. The kitten has 3 whiskers on the right and 3 on the left. How many whiskers does the kitten have? *Ans:* 6 whiskers.

30. Asha Patel is 5. She has 2 brothers and 3 sisters. How many children are in her family? *Ans:* 6 children.

    Solution: There is 1 Asha plus her 2 brothers and 3 sisters = 6 children.

31. I have 5 kittens and Kerry has none. How many kittens do we have together? *Ans:* 5 kittens.

32. A store has 2 aisles in the front and 3 in the back. How many aisles does the store have? *Ans:* 5 aisles.

33. There are 2 houses on the right bank of the river and 3 houses on the left. How many houses are on the river? *Ans:* 5 houses.

34. Hugo has 3 toy cars. How many more does he need to make 4? *Ans:* 1 car.

35. Nadia baked 2 pies. How many does she have to bake to make 4? *Ans:* 2 pies.

36. Henry got 4 yellow pencils and 1 red pencil. How many pencils does he have? *Ans:* 5 pencils.

37. Yoda was 3 feet tall and grew 2 more feet. How many feet is he now? *Ans:* 5 feet.

38. On the bus, there is 1 kid with a hat and 4 kids without hats. How many kids are on the bus? *Ans:* 5 kids.

39. My kitten caught 1 lizard, 2 snails and 2 flies. How many creatures did she catch? *Ans:* 5 creatures.

40. Being thirsty, Fiona drank 3 glasses of water, 2 glasses of lemonade, and 1 glass of juice. How many glasses did she drink? *Ans:* 6 glasses.

41. Old MacDonald had 2 cows and 4 chickens on his farm. How many animals did he have? *Ans:* 6 animals.

Addition up to 9

⇨ *When adding two numbers we can switch the order of the numbers and the sum will still be the same.*

Example
$3 + 4 = 7$ and $4 + 3 = 7$ $5 + 4 = 9$ and $4 + 5 = 9$

We can change places for all the number in addition and the answer will stay the same. Look:
$1 + 2 + 3 = 6$ $3 + 2 + 1 = 6$ $2 + 1 + 3 = 6$ $3 + 1 + 2 = 6$

Exercise I

Count forward to 19 staring with 0. Count backward from 19 down to 0.
Count backwards from 19 to 0 skipping every other number.
Count from 1 to 20, skipping every other number.
    Ans: 1, 3, 5, 7, 9, etc.

Exercise II

$5 + 1 = 6$	$6 + 2 = 8$	$6 + 1 = 7$	$7 + 2 = 9$	$4 + 4 = 8$
$6 + 1 = 7$	$2 + 6 = 8$	$1 + 6 = 7$	$2 + 7 = 9$	$1 + 7 = 8$
$5 + 2 = 7$	$4 + 2 = 6$	$6 + 2 = 8$	$2 + 4 = 6$	$8 + 1 = 9$
$5 + 3 = 8$	$4 + 1 = 5$	$1 + 5 = 6$	$5 + 2 = 7$	$4 + 5 = 9$
$2 + 5 = 7$	$4 + 2 = 6$	$1 + 6 = 7$	$4 + 3 = 7$	$5 + 4 = 9$
$6 + 1 = 7$	$5 + 1 = 6$	$2 + 6 = 8$	$3 + 5 = 8$	$4 + 4 = 8$
$6 + 2 = 8$	$5 + 2 = 7$	$3 + 6 = 9$	$3 + 6 = 9$	$3 + 3 = 6$
$6 + 3 = 9$	$4 + 2 = 6$	$1 + 8 = 9$	$6 + 2 = 8$	$2 + 2 = 4$
$6 + 2 = 8$	$2 + 4 = 6$	$2 + 7 = 9$	$4 + 5 = 9$	$4 + 5 = 9$
$7 + 1 = 8$	$2 + 5 = 7$	$3 + 6 = 9$	$2 + 7 = 9$	$3 + 4 = 7$
$7 + 2 = 9$	$5 + 2 = 7$	$4 + 5 = 9$	$5 + 3 = 8$	$7 + 2 = 9$
$5 + 1 = 6$	$3 + 2 = 5$	$5 + 3 = 8$	$8 + 1 = 9$	$7 + 1 = 8$
$5 + 2 = 7$	$5 + 2 = 7$	$7 + 2 = 9$	$7 + 2 = 9$	$3 + 4 = 7$
$5 + 3 = 8$	$5 + 1 = 6$	$7 + 0 = 7$	$6 + 3 = 9$	$3 + 5 = 8$

Problem: $3 + 3 + 3 = 9$
Solution: First add $3 + 3$ which is equal to 6, then add 6 and 3 together.

Exercise III

$4 + 2 + 2 = 8$	$4 + 2 + 0 = 6$	$4 + 4 + 1 = 9$	$0 + 1 + 2 + 3 = 6$	$1 + 2 + 3 = 6$
$5 + 1 + 2 = 8$	$3 + 4 + 1 = 8$	$2 + 3 + 4 = 9$	$6 + 1 + 2 = 9$	$2 + 3 + 2 = 7$
$6 + 2 + 1 = 9$	$1 + 2 + 3 = 6$	$5 + 2 + 1 = 8$	$2 + 2 + 2 = 6$	$3 + 3 + 3 = 9$
$2 + 3 + 3 = 8$	$1 + 2 + 1 = 4$	$3 + 1 + 3 = 7$	$2 + 6 + 1 = 9$	$1 + 2 + 5 = 8$

Exercise IV

What numbers come after 6 but before 9?   *Ans:* 7 and 8
What number comes after 3 but before 5?   *Ans:* 4
What number comes after 5 but before 7?   *Ans:* 6
What numbers come after 5 but before 8?   *Ans:* 6 and 7
What number added to 8 makes 9?   *Ans:* 1
What number added to 6 makes 9?   *Ans:* 3
What number added to 5 makes 9?   *Ans:* 4
What number added to 7 makes 9?   *Ans:* 2
What number added to 4 makes 9?   *Ans:* 5
What number added to 2 makes 9?   *Ans:* 7

Word Problems

1. There are 3 other people in John's family besides John. One day 2 friends came to dinner. How many plates did John put on the table for dinner that night? *Ans:* 6 plates. John has to eat too!

2. Four birds were sitting on a branch. Then 3 more came. How many birds are there now? *Ans:* 7 birds.

3. Usually, it takes 4 minutes for John to get ready, but today he spent 2 minutes more than usual. How long did it take him to get ready today? *Ans:* 6 minutes.

4. Puja has 5 dollars and she borrowed 2 more. How much money does she have? *Ans:* 7 dollars.

5. It's Dan's job to sweep the front steps every day. There are 3 steps in the front and 4 in the back. How many steps does he sweep every day? *Ans:* 7 steps.

6. Jill had 2 dolls. Her mom gave her 1 more and then her aunt gave her 2 more. How many dolls does she have now? *Ans:* 5 dolls.

7. How many towels would mother wash after she found 3 of Jane's dirty towels and 3 of Susan's dirty towels? *Ans:* 6 towels.

8. Victoria planted 1 cactus, 2 daisies and 3 pansies. How many plants did she plant? *Ans:* 6 plants.

9. Bob is 5 years old. How old will he be in 1 year? *Ans:* 6.
   a) In 2 years? *Ans:* 7.
   b) In 3 years? *Ans:* 8.
   c) In 4 years? *Ans:* 9.

10. A gardener worked 1 hour in the morning and 5 hours in the afternoon. How many hours did he work? *Ans:* 6 hours.

11. How many curtains will be needed for 5 windows in the kitchen and 3 windows in the dining room? *Ans:* 8 curtains.

12. Our house has 3 rooms upstairs and 4 downstairs. How many rooms are in our house? *Ans:* 7 rooms.

13. If John has 4 notebooks and Susan has 3 notebooks, how many notebooks do they have together? *Ans:* 7 notebooks.

14. In the living room, we have 2 sofas, 2 chairs and 3 tables. How many pieces of furniture are in the living room? *Ans:* 7 pieces.

15. Place 4 big glasses and 3 small ones on the table. How many glasses are on the table? *Ans:* 7 glasses.

16. I have 2 friends who live on my street and 4 friends who live far away. How many friends do I have? *Ans:* 6 friends.

17. Jen has 3 friends who are girls and 4 friends who are boys. How many friends does she have? *Ans:* 7 friends.

18. How many rolls does Curtis bake if he puts 4 in one pan and 4 in another? *Ans:* 8 rolls.

19. Tyron ate 3 eggs, Susan ate 1 egg and their dad ate 2 eggs. How many eggs did they all eat? *Ans:* 6 eggs.

20. Mom added 2 cups of sugar in the mix. Then she put 5 cups of flour. How many cups of ingredients did she add to the mix? *Ans:* 7 cups.

21. Angel's mom gave her 2 stars for picking up the plates, 2 stars for keeping her desk clean and 4 more stars for helping her brother. How many stars did Angel earn? *Ans:* 8 stars.

22. John washed 4 dogs, Susan washed 2 and Sam washed 2. How many dogs did they wash all together? *Ans:* 8 dogs.

23. Michael read 2 pages aloud, Victor read the next 2, and Nina read the last 3 pages of a story. How many pages did they read all together? *Ans:* 7 pages.

24. First 4 rosebuds bloomed. Then 4 more bloomed. How many buds are blooming? *Ans:* 8 buds.

25. If Jorge hung 7 birdfeeders in the backyard and Jose put up 2 more, how many birdfeeders are in the backyard? *Ans:* 9 birdfeeders.

26. A town has 3 benches in the park and plans to put 6 more. How many benches will be in the park then? *Ans:* 9 benches.

27. Our team scored 3 goals and the guest team scored 5. How many goals were scored in the game? *Ans:* 8 goals.

28. The bicycle shop sells 4 helmets each day. How many helmets did they sell yesterday and today? *Ans:* 8 helmets.

29. If a basketball team has 3 players and 6 more are coming, how many players will there be on the team? *Ans:* 9 players.

30. A poet wrote 3 poems in the morning and 5 poems in the afternoon and none in the evening. How many poems did she write for the whole day? *Ans:* 8 poems.

31. There are 4 rugs on the first floor and 3 rugs on the second floor in John's home. If he has to vacuum them all, how many rugs will he vacuum in all? *Ans:* 7 rugs.

32. There were 6 people on the bus when it picked up 3 more passengers. How many people are on the bus now? *Ans:* 9 people.

33. Four birds were sitting in a tree. Then 5 more came. How many birds are in the tree now? *Ans:* 9 birds.

34. Usually, John takes 7 minutes to get ready for school, but he spent 2 extra minutes brushing his teeth this morning. How long did it take for him to get ready? *Ans:* 9 minutes.

35. Mom took out $5 to pay for the vegetables but the farmer said, "You owe me $4 more." How much did the vegetables cost? *Ans:* $9.

36. Jennie opened 3 jars of plums, and Clara opened 5 jars. How many jars were opened? *Ans:* 8 jars.

37. John had 2 toy trucks and his aunt gave him 2 more; then his dad gave him 2 more trucks. How many trucks does he have now? *Ans:* 6 trucks.

38. How many chairs will we need to seat mom, dad, grandma and 4 kids at one table? *Ans:* 7 chairs.

39. Vic planted 1 rose, 2 daisies, and 3 pansies. How many flowers did he plant? *Ans:* 6 flowers.

40. There are 7 lamp posts on one side of the street and 2 on the other. How many are on both sides? *Ans:* 9 lamp posts.

41. Four plumbers worked 2 hours before lunch and 6 hours after lunch. How many total hours did they work?
    Ans: 8 hours. Remember to count hours, not plumbers.

42. Ann kept 4 crayons in one box and 5 in another. How many crayons are in both boxes? *Ans:* 9 crayons

43. If John has 3 awards and Susan has 4, how many awards do they have together? *Ans:* 7 awards.

44. I see 2 magazines on the sofa, 2 on the chair and 3 on the coffee table. How many magazines do I see? *Ans:* 7 magazines.

45. I scratched my nose 6 times with my right hand and 3 times with the left. How many times did I scratch my nose? *Ans:* 9 times.

46. How many pages did Emily write, if she wrote 2 pages today and 5 yesterday? *Ans:* 7 pages.

47. John ate 2 plums, Susan ate 1 and dad had 4. How many plums did they eat? *Ans:* 7 plums.

48. Henry had 6 quarters before his mother gave him 2 more. How many quarters does he have now? *Ans:* 8 quarters.

49. Tim lost 5 marbles, and then he lost 4 more. How many of his marbles did he lose? *Ans:* 9.

50. John found 4 golf balls, and Will and Andy found 2 each. How many golf balls did all three find? *Ans:* 8 balls.

    Solution: 4 balls that John found + 2 balls that Will found + 2 that Andy found = 8 balls.

51. If a jacket cost $5 and a pair of pants costs $4, what will they both cost? *Ans:* $9.

52. There are 6 eggs in one nest, and 2 in another. How many eggs are in both nests? *Ans:* 8 eggs.

53. George has 2 goldfish, and James has 7. How many goldfish do they both have? *Ans:* 9 goldfish.

54. A farmer had 3 chickens, and bought 5 more. How many chickens does he have now? *Ans:* 8 chickens.

55. This year our poodle had 4 puppies, last year she had 3 puppies and the year before only 1. How many puppies did she have altogether? *Ans:* 8 puppies.

56. There are 3 bars of soap in one box, 2 in another, and 3 more bars of soap in the third. How many bars of soap are there? *Ans:* 8 bars of soap.

57. There are 3 bottles of shampoo on one shelf, 3 on another, and 2 more on the third. How many bottles are there? *Ans:* 8 bottles.

58. Mom planted 4 daisies and 3 pansies. How many plants did she plant in the garden? *Ans:* 7 plants.

59. Mom had planted 7 plants and then she planted 2 more. How many plants are in the flower bed now? *Ans:* 9 plants.

60. Of the 9 plants, only 7 are flower plants. How many are not flower plants? *Ans:* 2 plants. What kind of plants might they be?

Subtraction with numbers up to 6

Subtraction is the opposite of addition. When we subtract from a number, we take away from that number. We can also use subtraction to find the difference between two numbers.

Exercise I

Count backward from 6 by 1 (i.e. 6, 5, 4)
Count backward from 6 by 2 (i.e. 6, 4, 2, and 0)
Count backward from 6 by 3 (i.e. 6, 3, and 0)

⇨ *In subtraction the order is very important!*
   3 take away 1 equals 2, but 1 take away 2 does not equal 3! Later on we will learn how to take away a big number from a small. But now, let's subtract, or take away, only from bigger or equal numbers.

Exercise II

3 - 2 = 1	6 - 4 = 2	5 - 0 = 5	6 - 1 = 5	5 - 2 = 3
4 - 2 = 2	6 - 6 = 0	3 - 0 = 3	6 - 2 = 4	6 - 2 = 4
5 - 2 = 3	6 - 5 = 1	1 - 1 = 0	6 - 3 = 3	4 - 2 = 2
3 - 3 = 0	5 - 2 = 3	2 - 1 = 1	6 - 2 = 4	5 - 1 = 4
4 - 3 = 1	5 - 4 = 1	6 - 2 = 4	6 - 4 = 2	6 - 4 = 2
5 - 3 = 2	5 - 3 = 2	6 - 1 = 5	2 - 2 = 0	4 - 2 = 2
6 - 2 = 4	5 - 2 = 3	3 - 1 = 2	6 - 3 - 3 = 0	4 - 3 = 1
6 - 3 = 3	5 - 5 = 0	6 - 3 = 3	6 - 3 - 2 = 1	4 - 1 = 3

Exercise III

What number do you take away from 4 to make 3?	*Ans:* 1
What number do you take away from 4 to make 2?	*Ans:* 2
What number do you take away from 3 to make 1?	*Ans:* 2
What number do you take away from 2 to make 0?	*Ans:* 2
What number do you take away from 5 to make 4?	*Ans:* 1
What number do you take away from 5 to make 3?	*Ans:* 2
What number do you take away from 5 to make 1?	*Ans:* 4
What number do you take away from 6 to make 6?	*Ans:* 0
What number do you take away from 6 to make 3?	*Ans:* 3

What number do you take away from 6 to make 4?   *Ans:* 2
What number do you take away from 6 to make 2?   *Ans:* 4
What number do you take away from 4 to make 1?   *Ans:* 3

Word Problems

1.   Four birds were sitting on the branch, then 2 flew away. How many birds stayed on the branch? *Ans:* 2 birds.

2.   A family put aside 3 hours to clean the yard. They worked for 2 hours. How much longer will they work? *Ans:* 1 hour.

3.   The story is 5 pages long. I read 2 pages. How many pages are left? *Ans:* 3 pages.

4.   Our team scored 5 points. The guest team scored 3. How many points will it take for the guest team to tie the game? *Ans:* 2 points.

    Solution: It takes altogether 5 points to tie the game for the guests. They already have 3, then 5 - 3 = 2. It will take 2 points for the other team to tie the game.

5.   There were 3 delicious apples on the table. I ate 2 and my little sister ate 1. How many apples are left for my older brother? *Ans:* 0 apples.

6.   There were only 5 pretty rosebuds on the bush. Jane cut 2 of these to take to her teacher. How many rosebuds are there on the plant? *Ans:* 3 rosebuds.

7.   A sailor saw 4 seagulls and 2 pelicans. How many more seagulls than pelicans did the sailor see? *Ans:* 2 seagulls.

8.   There were 6 strings on my guitar. Jerry broke 2 of the strings today. How many strings are left for him to break? *Ans:* 4 strings.

9.   Our cat had 4 kittens. 3 of the kittens are brown and the rest gray. How many are not brown? *Ans:* 1 kitten.

10.   There are 6 plates in a dinner set. Today, 4 people sat for dinner. How many plates stayed in the cabinet? *Ans:* 2 plates.

11.   Mark promised to replace 6 light bulbs in the classroom. He replaced 3. How many more does he need to replace to keep his promise? *Ans:* 3 lightbulbs.

12.   Chris takes care of 5 lemon trees. He watered 4 of them. How many are left for him to water? *Ans:* 1 tree.

13. The Martinez family has 6 children. 5 are in college, away from home. How many children are still at home? *Ans:* 1 child.

14. Jim's company has 5 trucks. One truck is on the road. How many are in the garage? *Ans:* 4 trucks.

15. Erica brought 6 pencils for the test. She gave 2 pencils to Monica and 1 pencil to Phil. How many pencils does she have now? *Ans:* 3 pencils (6 - 2 = 4, then 4 - 1 = 3).

16. Chloe took out 5 eggs to make a cake. She dropped 1 on the floor and used 1 for baking. How many eggs did she put back in the fridge? *Ans:* 3 eggs.

17. I tried to call my grandparents 4 times this week. The number was busy 2 of the times. How many times did I get through? *Ans:* 2 times.

18. Katie's porch has 5 steps. Her puppy climbed up 3 steps. How many more steps does the puppy need to climb to get to the top? *Ans:* 2 steps.

19. There were 5 plums on the counter. My sister and I ate 1 each. How many plums are still on the counter? *Ans:* 3 plums.

20. There were 6 crayons in the box. Connor took out 1 red crayon and 1 blue crayon. How many crayons are left in the box? *Ans:* 4 crayons.

21. Kelly brought 4 presents for her friends to school. One friend had a dentist appointment and missed school that day. How many friends got their presents? *Ans:* 3 friends.

22. Lucy planted 3 trees and Missy planted 6. How many more trees did Missy plant than Lucy? *Ans:* 3 trees.

23. Olga swam 5 laps in the pool. Tim swam 2 laps less than Olga. How many laps did Tim swim? *Ans:* 3 laps.

24. Leah paid for a book with a 5 dollar bill and received $1 in change. How much did the book cost? *Ans:* $4.

25. A school bus has 6 seats. 4 students are on the bus. How many seats are empty? *Ans:* 2 seats.

26. Doris can do 4 pushups. Her friend can do only 2. How many more pushups can Doris do? *Ans:* 2 pushups more than her friend.

27. Tess can cross her driveway in 6 hops. She stopped after 2 hops. How many more hops she has left to the other side? *Ans:* 4 hops.

28. There were 5 people at the bus stop. Now, there are only 2. How many people got on the bus? *Ans:* 3 people.

29. My one-year-old baby niece has 6 teeth. Last time I saw her she had 2 teeth. How many new teeth did she grow?
    Ans: 4 new teeth.

30. A bug has 6 legs and 2 wings. How many more legs than wings does the bug have? *Ans:* 4 more legs than wings.

31. There were 4 T-shirts lying on the sofa. Dad picked up 1 and Steve picked up 3. How many T-shirts are on the sofa now?
    Ans: 0 or none. Always pick up your T-shirts.

32. Harold put 6 cherries on his plate, but now there are only 5. How many cherries are missing? *Ans:* 1 cherry.

33. A black sheep gave the master 3 bags of wool. One went to the master and one for the dame. How many were left for a boy down the lane?
    Ans: 1 bag.

34. Morris has $3. How much does he need to borrow to make $5? *Ans:* $2.

35. The team has 4 players. How many more does it need to make 6?
    Ans: 2 players.

36. For the concert I learned 2 songs. How many more songs do I need to learn to make it 6? *Ans:* 4 songs.

37. Julia is 6 years old.
    a) How old was she 3 years ago? *Ans:* 3 years old.
    b) How old was she 2 years ago? *Ans:* 4 years old.
    c) How old was she 4 years ago? *Ans:* 2 years old.

38. Edward did 4 lessons in the morning, and then 3 in the afternoon. How many lessons did he do altogether? *Ans:* 7 lessons.

39. There are 5 birds sitting on a branch. 2 flew away. How many are on the branch now? *Ans:* 3 birds.

40. Susan bought 6 yards of fabric at one store, and 3 yards at another. How many yards does she have now? *Ans:* 9 yards.

41. Mother gave Harry $6. Harry's sister borrowed $2 from him. How much does he have now? *Ans:* $4.

42. Alan ate 4 oranges, and Arthur ate 3. How many oranges did they both eat? *Ans:* 7 oranges.

43. Ella paid 3 coins for a pencil, and 5 coins for a notebook. How much did she pay for both? *Ans:* 8 coins.

44. There are 5 pears on one branch, 2 are ripe. How many pears are still green? *Ans:* 3 pears.

45. Alice ate 4 carrots, and her mom also ate 4. How many carrots did they both eat? *Ans:* 8. Carrots are good for kids and grown ups.

46. Ella picked 4 bags of cherries, and Joseph picked 4. How many bags did they both pick? *Ans:* 8 bags.

47. A farmer planted 6 acres of land. 2 acres grow potatoes, and the rest have corn. How many acres grow corn? *Ans:* 4 acres.

48. Anna made 6 pies, and her family ate 4 of them the same day. How many pies are left? *Ans:* 2 pies.

49. One man can dig 6 holes and another can fill 3 in one day. How many holes will be there at the end of the day if one digs and the other fills? *Ans:* 3 holes.

50. There are 4 horses in one pasture, and 5 in another. How many horses are in both? *Ans:* 9 horses.

51. Jasper had 6 books and gave away 2. How many books he has now? *Ans:* 4 books.

52. If a goldfish is worth $2 and a starfish $4, how much would both cost? *Ans:* $6.

53. The family caught 5 fish and ate 3 that night. How many were left for next day? *Ans:* 2 fish.

54. A short and stout little teapot had 5 cups of tea in it. It poured out 4 cups. How many cups of tea does it still have? *Ans:* 1 cup.

Addition up to 10

Exercise I

Count from 30 to 100.
Can you count backwards from 100 to 30?

Exercise II

2 + 1 = 3	4 + 4 = 8	2 + 5 = 7	3 + 4 = 7	4 + 5 = 9
2 + 2 = 4	4 + 5 = 9	1 + 6 = 7	3 + 5 = 8	3 + 4 = 7
3 + 2 = 5	5 + 2 = 7	1 + 7 = 8	4 + 5 = 9	3 + 7 = 10
2 + 3 = 5	6 + 2 = 8	2 + 6 = 8	2 + 7 = 9	2 + 7 = 9
3 + 3 = 6	7 + 2 = 9	3 + 5 = 8	5 + 2 = 7	3 + 7 = 10
3 + 4 = 7	7 + 1 = 8	5 + 4 = 9	0 + 7 = 7	5 + 5 = 10
4 + 2 = 6	8 + 1 = 9	5 + 5 = 10	9 + 1 = 10	10 + 0 = 10
2 + 4 = 6	8 + 2 = 10	6 + 4 = 10	8 + 2 = 10	3 + 4 = 7
4 + 3 = 7	7 + 3 = 10	5 + 5 = 10	7 + 2 = 9	2 + 7 = 9
4 + 4 = 8	3 + 3 = 6	5 + 4 = 9	7 + 3 = 10	4 + 5 = 9
3 + 3 = 6	5 + 2 = 7	4 + 4 = 8	6 + 3 = 9	3 + 4 = 7
3 + 5 = 8	1 + 6 = 7	8 + 1 = 9	6 + 4 = 10	5 + 4 = 9
3 + 6 = 9	3 + 4 = 7	7 + 2 = 9	4 + 4 = 8	6 + 3 = 9
4 + 3 = 7	4 + 3 = 7	6 + 3 = 9	5 + 5 = 10	7 + 3 = 10

Exercise III

While asking addition questions, this exercise uses subtraction to solve the problems.

What number do you add to 4 to make 9?	*Ans:* 5
What number do you add to 5 to make 8?	*Ans:* 3
What number do you add to 4 to make 8?	*Ans:* 4
What number do you add to 3 to make 9?	*Ans:* 6
What number do you add to 9 to make 9?	*Ans:* 0
What number do you add to 2 to make 7?	*Ans:* 5
What number do you add to 1 to make 7?	*Ans:* 6
What number do you add to 4 to make 7?	*Ans:* 3
What number do you add to 6 to make 9?	*Ans:* 3
What number do you add to 3 to make 8?	*Ans:* 5

Word Problems

1.   A lady bought 6 red pens and 4 blue pens. How many pens did she buy? *Ans:* 10 pens.

2.   In a class there are 3 boys and 6 girls. How many students are in the class? *Ans:* 9 students.

3.   There are 7 doves on one tree, and 3 doves on another. How many doves are there? *Ans:* 10 doves.

4.   A coat cost $8, and a pair of boots $2. What was the cost of both? *Ans:* $10.

5.   I planted 7 lemon trees and 2 apple trees. How many trees did I plant? *Ans:* 9 trees.

6.   Robert stayed with his aunt for 4 days and with his uncle for 6 days. How many days did he stay with both? *Ans:* 10 days.

7.   Fred has 5 ducks and his brother has 2. How many ducks do they both own? *Ans:* 7 Ducks. Quack!

8.   Walter had 6 coins and found 2 more. How many coins does he have now? *Ans:* 8 coins.

9.   Rose worked on 7 problems, and Lily worked on 3. How many problems did they both do? *Ans:* 10 problems.

10. Isaac earned 6 dimes, and then gave 3 to Kate. How many dimes does he have now? *Ans:* 3 dimes.

11. Lewis fed his horse 2 ears of corn on Friday, and 5 ears on Saturday. How many ears of corn did the horse eat? *Ans:* 7 ears of corn.

12. I hid 2 books under the table and 6 books under the sofa. How many books did I hide? *Ans:* 8 books.

13. I got 2 scratches from the bush and 3 from falling on the ground. How many scratches did I get? *Ans:* 5 scratches.

14. I am 6 years old.
     a) How old will I be in 3 years? *Ans:* 9 years old.
     b) How old will I be in 4 years? *Ans:* 10 years old.
     c) How old was I 2 years ago? *Ans:* 4 years old.
     d) How old was I 6 years ago? *Ans:* 0 years old.

15. I have 2 brothers and 3 sisters. How many kids are in my family? *Ans:* 6 kids (me + 2 + 3).

16. I practiced piano for 2 hours, guitar for 1 hour, and drums for 3 hours. How many hours did I play music all together? *Ans:* 6 hours.

17. Jack has 7 trucks and Joey has none. How many trucks do they have together? *Ans:* 7 trucks.

18. Ann washed 8 dishes and her brother washed 2. How many dishes did they wash together? *Ans:* 10 dishes.

19. There are 2 shelves on the wall. Each shelf has 4 glasses. How many glasses are there? *Ans:* 8 glasses (4 + 4 = 8).

20. If a ruler cost $2, a pencil $1, and a notebook $5, what will all three cost? *Ans:* $8.

21. There are 3 eggs in one nest, and 4 in another. How many eggs are in both? *Ans:* 7 eggs.

22. Tricia has 2 toy trains, and James has 7. How many trains do they both have? *Ans:* 9 trains.

23. A farmer had 5 horses and bought 4 more. How many has he now? *Ans:* 9 horses.

24. Emily found 2 pine cones, and her sister found 6. How many did they both find? *Ans:* 8 pine cones.

25. There are 5 bars of soap in one box, and 2 in another. How many bars are in both? *Ans:* 7 bars.

26. Jen is 3 years old.
    a) What will be her age in 3 years from now? *Ans:* 6 years old.
    b) How old will she be in 5 years? *Ans:* 8 years old.
    c) How old will she be in 7 years? *Ans:* 10 years old.

27. Ali did 4 lessons in the morning, and 3 in the afternoon. How many lessons did he do? *Ans:* 7 lessons.

28. There are 2 birds in my hands, and 7 in the bush. How many birds are there? *Ans:* 9 birds.

29. Susan bought 6 cookies in one store, and 2 in another. How many cookies does she have now? *Ans:* 8 cookies.

30. Talia's father gave her $3, and her mother gave her $7. How much money does she have? *Ans:* 10 dollars.

31. Alan bought 5 oranges, and Bertha bought 3. How many did they both buy? *Ans:* 8 oranges.

32. There are 2 chairs in the room. One chair has 4 legs and the other also has 4 legs. How many legs are on both chairs? *Ans:* 8 legs.

33. Mary picked 5 roses, and Emma picked 4. How many did they both pick? *Ans:* 9 roses.

34. Little Jack Horner stuck his fingers into a pie and pulled out 3 plums. Then he did it again and got out 5 plums. How many plums did he get? *Ans:* 8 plums.

35. A jacket has 2 pockets. There is $5 in each pocket. How much money is in both? *Ans:* 10 dollars.

36. Erik had 5 electric cars and broke 4. How many working cars does he have now? *Ans:* 1 car.

37. There are 7 rugs upstairs and 2 rugs downstairs. If I vacuumed them all, how many would be clean? *Ans:* 9 rugs.

38. The secret password has 4 letters and 5 numbers. How many letters and numbers are in the password? *Ans:* 9 letters and numbers.

39. How many two-number combinations together will make 10?
Ans: 6 combinations. *Ans:* $1 + 9 = 10$, $2 + 8 = 10$, $3 + 7 = 10$, $4 + 6 = 10$, $5 + 5 = 10$. And don't forget that $10 + 0$ also makes 10.

40. Jack had 8 candies. His mom gave him 2 more. How many does he have now? *Ans:* 10 candies.

41. Jill had 4 candies and Jack gave her 6 more. How many does she have? *Ans:* 10 candies.

42. I have 3 white shirts and 3 black shirts in my suitcase. How many black and white shirts do I have? *Ans:* 6 shirts.

43. There are 4 boys and 4 girls in the room. How many kids are in the room? *Ans:* 8 kids.

44. I had 2 safety pins and then I got 8 more. How many pins do I have now? *Ans:* 10 pins.

45. I hold 3 coins in one hand and 6 coins in the other. How many coins do I have? *Ans:* 9 coins.

46. Mary's mom told her to take 2 apples from the table and 6 apples from the pantry to make a pie. How many apples did Mary get? *Ans:* 8 apples.

47. Annie put 2 coins on the table, her brother put 8 more. How many coins are on the table? *Ans:* 10 coins.

48. Jill ate 1 plum, 3 apples and 5 cookies. How many "things" did she eat? *Ans:* 9 "things".

49. Camilla has 4 red dresses, 4 yellow dresses and 1 green dress. How many dresses does she have? *Ans:* 9 dresses.

50. I put 4 grapes on a plate. Then I put 3 more grapes. How many grapes are on the plate? *Ans:* 7 grapes.

51. I have 3 friends and then 3 more kids become my friends. How many friends do I have now? *Ans:* 6 friends.

52. There are 7 boys and 2 girls in the room. How many kids are in the room? **Ans:** 9 kids.

53. I had 7 balls and then I got 3 more. How many balls do I have now? **Ans:** 10 balls.

54. I hold 5 coins in one hand and 4 coins in the other. How many coins do I have? **Ans:** 9 coins.

Digits and Place Value

Parent: Please read this section with your child.

The numbers 1, 2, 3, 4, 5, 6, 7, 8, 9 and the number 0 are called digits. Numbers are made up of digits. Example: Number 23 is made up of two digits.

Reading from left to right, where a digit is in a number is important. The location of the digit is called its place value. Example: Number 45 has two digits. The digit 4 and digit 5 have different place value.

We can think of numbers as sitting in chairs. A one-digit number needs just one chair. A two-digit number (like 12 or 32) takes 2 chairs and a 3 digit number has 3 chairs for its three digits.

```
                                3
                             2  3
                          4  2  3
```

100 10' 1's

The numbers can be described by the number of digits. For example: number 3 has only one digit and is called a one-digit number.

Number 16 has two digits (1 and 6) and is called a two-digit number. Sometimes two-digit numbers are also called double-digit numbers.

Number 254 has 3 digits (2, 5, and 4) and is called a three or triple-digit number.

There are also four, five, six, and more digit numbers.

Each digit place has its "value." A one-digit number, like 3, has only ones place.

Two digit numbers, like 23, have places for ones and tens. The tens place has a higher value than ones. It's worth more. In number 23, digit 2 sits in the chair for tens. In ones chair sits 3.

To figure out what other numbers a number is made up of, we take the digit in the tens place and multiply it by 10. For 23, it is 2 x 10 = 20. The last number is just 3. That means that the whole number is made of 20 and 3. In other words, you can think of number 23 as 20 + 3.

A three digit number, like 423, has places for ones, tens, and hundreds. That means that 4 is in the hundreds place and this chair holds 4 one hundreds. 2 is in tens place with the chair that is worth 20, and 3 is in ones place with the chair that holds 3. We can also show it this way.

423 = $\underline{100 + 100 + 100 + 100} + \underline{10 + 10} + \underline{1 + 1 + 1}$

One digit numbers like 1, 2, 3, 4, 5, 6, 7, 8, and 9 all make their home in value place for ones.

We say, for example, that number 23 has 3 in ones place and number 2 in tens place.

Numbers one through nine have only one-digit and it is in the ones place. After number nine comes 10, a two-digit number. The place in front of the ones is tens place. We can say that 10 has "1" sitting in the tens place and "0" in the ones place.

Remember: 0 is a digit.

For number 12: 1 is in the tens place and 2 is in the ones place
In number 20: 2 is in the tens place and zero is in the ones place
In number 45: 4 is in the tens place and 5 is in the ones place
In number 33: 3 is in the tens place and 3 is in the ones place
In three-digit numbers, like 100, we say the one is in the hundreds place, zero in the tens place and zero is in the ones place.
In number 123: 1 is in the hundreds place and 2 is in the tens place and 3 in the ones place.
In number 207: 2 is in the hundreds place, zero is in the tens place and 7 in the ones place.
In number 845: 8 is in the hundreds place, 4 is in the tens place and 5 in the ones place.
In number 333: 3 is in the hundreds place, 3 is in the tens place and 3 in the ones place.

Exercise I

All numbers are made up from single digit numbers. Number 10 has ten ones in it. Number 20 has two 10s in it. Each of these tens has ten ones in it.

Ten tens make one hundred, written 100.

11 is made of 1 ten and 1 one
12 is made of 1 ten and 2 ones
13 is made of 1 ten and 3 ones

What do the following numbers mean?
46 is made of how many tens and ones? *Ans:* 4 tens and 6 ones
63 is made of how many tens and ones? *Ans:* 6 tens and 3 ones
50 is made of how many tens and ones? *Ans:* 5 tens and 0 ones
29 is made of how many tens and ones? *Ans:* 2 tens and 9 ones
31 is made of how many tens and ones? *Ans:* 3 tens and 1 one

Exercise II

What number do three tens and five ones make? *Ans:* 35
What number do four tens and five ones make? *Ans:* 45
What number do six tens and seven ones make? *Ans:* 67
What number do five tens and nine ones make? *Ans:* 59
What number do seven tens make? *Ans:* 70
What number do four tens and three ones make? *Ans:* 43

Word Problems

1. In number 19, what is in the tens place and what is in the ones?
    Ans: One is in the tens place and 7 is in the ones place.

2. In number 23, what is in the tens place and what is in the ones?
    Ans: 2 is in the tens place and 3 is in the ones place.

3. In number 32, what is in the tens place and what is in the ones?
    Ans: 3 is in the tens place and 2 is in the ones place.

4. In number 60, what is in the tens place and what is in the ones?
    Ans: 6 is in the tens place and 0 is in the ones place.

5. In number 99, what is in the tens place and what is in the ones?
    Ans: 9 is in the tens place and 9 is in the ones place.

6. In number 16, what is in the tens place and what is in the ones?
    Ans: 1 is in the tens place and 6 is in the ones place.

7. In 3 digit numbers like 124, 4 is in the ones place, and 2 is in the tens place. What number is in the hundreds place? *Ans:* 1 is in hundreds place.

8. In number 157, what is in the hundreds place, in the tens place, and in the ones? *Ans:* One is in the hundreds, 5 is in the tens and 7 is in the ones place.

9. In number 321, what is in the hundreds place, in the tens place, and in the ones? *Ans:* 3 is in the hundreds, 2 is in the tens and 1 is in the ones place.

10. In number 842, what is in the hundreds place, in the tens place, and in the ones? *Ans:* 8 is in the hundreds, 4 is in the tens and 2 is in the ones place.

11. In number 898, what is in the hundreds place, in the tens place, and in the ones? *Ans:* 8 is in the hundreds, 9 is in the tens, and 8 is in the ones place.

12. In number 204, what is in the tens place? *Ans:* 0 is in the tens place.

13. In number 321, what is in the tens place? *Ans:* 2 is in the tens place.

14. In number 571, what is in the ones place? *Ans:* 1 is in the ones place.

15. In number 50, what is in the tens place? *Ans:* 5 is in the tens place.

Subtraction with numbers up to 10

Exercise I

Count backward from 10 by 1 (i.e., 10, 11, 12, etc.)
Count backward from 10 by 2 (i.e., 10, 8, 6, etc.)
Count backward from 10 by 3 (i.e., 10, 7, 4, and 1)
Count backward from 10 by 4 (i.e., 10, 6, and 2)

Exercise II

7 - 1 = 6	7 - 5 = 2	9 - 7 = 2	9 - 6 - 2 = 1
7 - 2 = 5	6 - 5 = 1	8 - 4 = 4	9 - 5 - 2 = 2
7 - 3 = 4	8 - 6 = 2	9 - 5 = 4	9 - 2 - 2 = 5
7 - 2 = 5	7 - 6 = 1	9 - 4 = 5	9 - 4 - 5 = 0
7 - 5 = 2	8 - 3 = 5	9 - 3 = 6	10 - 2 = 8
7 - 1 - 1 = 5	9 - 9 = 0	9 - 2 = 7	10 - 3 = 7
7 - 2 - 1 = 4	9 - 8 = 1	8 - 2 - 1 = 5	10 - 5 = 5
7 - 2 - 2 = 3	8 - 2 - 2 = 4	8 - 3 - 1 = 4	10 - 9 = 1
7 - 4 - 2 = 1	8 - 2 - 1 = 5	9 - 1 - 1 = 7	10 - 4 = 6
7 - 5 - 1 = 1	8 - 1 - 3 = 4	9 - 1 - 2 = 6	10 - 8 = 2
7 - 4 - 1 = 2	8 - 3 - 2 = 3	9 - 2 - 3 = 4	10 - 1 = 9
7 - 2 - 3 = 2	8 - 3 - 1 = 4	9 - 3 - 3 = 3	10 - 2 = 8
8 - 1 = 7	8 - 3 - 4 = 1	9 - 4 - 2 = 3	8 - 4 - 2 - 1 = 1
8 - 2 = 6	8 - 4 - 4 = 0	9 - 2 - 5 = 2	7 - 3 - 2 - 1 = 1
8 - 3 = 5	8 - 3 - 4 = 1	9 - 3 - 1 = 5	7 - 2 - 2 - 1 = 2
8 - 7 = 1	8 - 5 - 1 = 2	9 - 4 - 3 = 2	10 - 7 = 3

Exercise III

What number do you take away from 9 to make 8? *Ans:* 1
What number do you take away from 10 to make 8? *Ans:* 2
What number do you take away from 8 to make 5? *Ans:* 3
What number do you take away from 8 to make 3? *Ans:* 5
What number do you take away from 9 to make 6? *Ans:* 3
What number do you take away from 9 to make 4? *Ans:* 5
What number do you take away from 7 to make 5? *Ans:* 2

What number do you take away from 8 to make 4?   *Ans:* 4
What number do you take away from 10 to make 6?   *Ans:* 4
What number do you take away from 10 to make 5?   *Ans:* 5
What number do you take away from 8 to make 2?   *Ans:* 6
What number do you take away from 10 to make 3?   *Ans:* 7

Exercise IV

What two numbers added together make 4?
  Ans: 1 and 3; 2 and 2; 4 and 0.
What two numbers added together make 5?
  Ans: 1 and 4; or 2 and 3; or 5 and 0.
What two numbers added together make 6?
  Ans: 1 and 5; 2 and 4; 3 and 3; 0 and 6.
What two numbers added together make 7?
  Ans: 1 and 6; 2 and 5; 3 and 4; 0 and 7.
What two numbers added together make 8?
  Ans: 1 and 7; 2 and 6; 3 and 5; 4 and 4; 0 and 8.
What two numbers added together make 9?
  Ans: 1 and 8; 2 and 7; 3 and 6; 4 and 5; 0 and 9.

Word Problems

1. Out of 6 cherry trees in the park, only 2 are blooming. How many more will bloom later? *Ans:* 4 trees.

2. Out of 8 students in our school band, 3 are girls. How many boys are there in the band? *Ans:* 5 boys.

3. A pet store had 8 fish in the tank and sold 6. How many fish are left for sale? *Ans:* 2 fish.

4. Ten girls came to Laura's birthday party. After the birthday cake, 5 girls went home and the rest stayed for a sleep-over. How many girls slept over? *Ans:* 5 girls.

5. It takes 9 minutes to walk to school but only 3 minutes to go by bicycle. How much longer does it take to walk to school than to ride the bicycle? *Ans:* 6 minutes.

6. Not counting the tails, Jay's hamster is 2 inches shorter than his pet bird. The bird is 8 inches long. How long is the hamster? *Ans:* 6 inches.

    Solution: The bird is 8 inches and the hamster is 2 inches less.
    Then, 8 inches - 2 inches = 6 inches.

7. Nash accidentally dropped 10 marbles. He looked but only found 8. How many of his marbles did he lose? *Ans:* 2 marbles.

8. We cut pizza into 8 pieces. Then we ate 4 pieces for lunch. How many pieces of pizza are left? *Ans:* 4 pieces.

9. It took Sherlock Holmes 6 minutes to get out of the maze. It took Doctor Watson 4 minutes longer. How long did it take for Dr. Watson to get out of the maze? *Ans:* 10 minutes.

10. Five out of my 7 wishes came true. How many more wishes are left to come true? *Ans:* 2 wishes.

11. Erika and Gail together bought 10 stickers. Erika bought 7. How many stickers did Gail buy? *Ans:* 3 stickers.

12. My aunt works 8 hours a day. She works 4 hours before lunch. How many hours does she work after lunch? *Ans:* 4 hours.

13. There are 8 seats at the table. 5 people sat down. How many empty seats are left? *Ans:* 3 seats.

14. The mystery writer always writes 8 pages a day. This morning she wrote only 1. How many more pages does she need to write before the day is over? *Ans:* 7 pages.

15. There are 9 potatoes in the bag. I took out 3. How many are in the bag now? *Ans:* 6 potatoes.

16. This week it rained for 3 days. How many days were without rain? *Ans:* 4 Hint: a week has 7 days.

17. Tuesday and Thursday are two days of the week that start with the letter "T". How many days of the week start with a letter other than "T"? *Ans:* 5 days. Can you name them? Monday, Wednesday, Friday, Saturday, Sunday.

18. In the classroom with 7 windows, 2 windows are open. How many windows are closed? *Ans:* 5 windows.

19. My father is 6 feet tall. I am only 4 feet tall. How much taller is my father? *Ans:* 2 feet, but I am growing.

20. Chip had $10 but spent $4. How much money does he have left? *Ans:* $6.

21. There are 7 miles between my house and the lake. I hiked 5 miles to the lake but got tired. How many more miles are left to walk before I get there? *Ans:* 2 miles.

22. Arthur has basketball practice at 9 o'clock. It is 6 o'clock now. How much time does he have before practice? *Ans:* 3 hours.

23. There were 8 shirts in the closet; 3 shirts are being washed and 1 is at the drycleaner. How many shirts are in the closet now? *Ans:* 4 shirts (8 - 3 = 5, then 5 - 1 = 4).

24. Mom bought 7 postage stamps and used 2 yesterday and another 2 today. How many stamps are left? *Ans:* 3 stamps (7 - 2 = 5, then 5 - 2 = 3).

25. Fay picked 7 apples off the ground and 2 from the tree. How many apples did she pick? *Ans:* 9 apples. She has to wash them before eating.

26. Playing 8 games in a chess tournament, Darla lost 3 and tied 3 games. How many games did she win? *Ans:* 2 games (8 - 3 = 5, then 5 - 3 = 2).

27. Gordon threw a dart 9 times and scored 6 times. How many times did he miss? *Ans:* 3 times.

28. There were 7 sparrows on a tree. First, 3 flew away and then 4 more flew away. How many sparrows are on the tree now? *Ans:* 0 sparrows.

29. Uncle Jim planned to take his 9 hats on the river cruise but took only 5 of them.
    a) How many hats did he leave at home? *Ans:* 4 hats.
    b) On the cruise, the wind blew off 2 of his hats. How many hats did the wind spare? *Ans:* 3 hats (remember, he took 5 hats on the cruise, 5 - 2 = 3).
    c) At a sea port he bought 6 new hats. How many hats does he have for the rest of his cruise? *Ans:* 9 hats (3 old hats + 6 new hats = 9 hats).

30. The school principal received 9 messages and returned 6. How many more messages are waiting to be returned? *Ans:* 3 messages.

31. There were 10 cartons of milk on the store shelf. The store sold 7. How many cartons are on the shelf now? *Ans:* 3 cartons.

32. Harry has to brush his teeth every day. This week he forgot to brush his teeth twice. How many times did Harry brush this whole week? *Ans:* 5 times. Your dentist won't be happy, Harry!

33. Michelle learned 7 new spelling words. On the test she spelled 5 correctly. How many words did she spell incorrectly? *Ans:* 2 words.

34. Jake washed his 7 T-shirts and 3 of his dad's. How many T-shirts did he wash? *Ans:* 10 shirts.

35. Sam gave the store clerk a 10 dollar bill. The store clerk gave him back $4 in change. How much money did Sam spend in the store? *Ans:* $6.

36. Rashid ran a mile in 10 minutes, his sister Reja did it in 7 minutes. How much longer did it take Rashid to run the mile? *Ans:* 3 minutes longer.

37. Last month we bought 9 jars of jam. Today, we only have 2 jars left. How many jars did we eat already? *Ans:* 7 jars. A bit too much, don't you think?

38. A group of 10 children went for a trip. Some children went home early from their trip and there were only 8 left. How many children went home early? *Ans:* 2 children.

39. A group of 9 children went to see a play. 3 kids sat in the balcony and the rest sat in the orchestra section. How many sat in the orchestra section? *Ans:* 6 children.

40. Misha picked 7 puppies out of 10. How many puppies didn't he pick? *Ans:* 3 puppies.

41. Tristan bought 9 pens and kept 5. He gave away the rest. How many pens did he give away? *Ans:* 4 pens.

42. Jake needs 10 stars to get a prize from his dad. He has 7 stars already. How many more does he need to earn? *Ans:* 3 stars.

43. Samuel took 6 books to school and then 4 more. How many books did he take to school? *Ans:* 10 books.

44. We had 9 eggs and we used 4 to make the cake. How many eggs are left? *Ans:* 5 eggs.

45. Marta was sent to the store with 8 dollars to buy medicine that costs 5 dollars. How much change will she bring back? *Ans:* $3.

46. The phone number has 10 digits. If the phone number is seven digits, how many digits are in the area code? *Ans:* 3 digits.

47. The phone number has 10 digits. If three digits are the area code, how many numbers make the rest? *Ans:* 7 numbers.

48. I set the table for 9 people but only 4 came. How many seats were empty? *Ans:* 5 seats.

49. The store has 10 T-shirts. 2 are white, 3 are black and the rest are yellow. How many yellow T-shirts does the store have? *Ans:* 5 yellow T-shirts.

50. The kitchen table has 7 chairs. There are 4 people in our family. How many chairs are not used? *Ans:* 3 chairs.

51. The carton has 8 cups of milk and we drank 5. How many cups of milk are left? *Ans:* 3 cups.

52. A cherry tree is 8 feet tall. A peach tree is 5 feet tall. How much taller is the cherry tree? *Ans:* 3 feet.

53. My mom is 5 feet tall. My dad is 6 feet tall. How much shorter is my mom than my dad? *Ans:* 1 foot.

54. Pauline picked 9 flowers. She gave 4 to her sister, 4 to her brother, and kept the rest. How many flowers did she keep? *Ans:* 1 flower.

Bonus problem:
55. Elizabeth, Elspeth, Betsey, and Bess all went together to find a bird's nest. They found a bird's nest with 5 eggs in it. They all picked one, and still there were 4 eggs left in the nest. How can that be? *Ans:* Elizabeth, Elspeth, Betsey, and Bess are the names and nicknames of the same person.

Lesson 9

Addition and subtraction up to 10

Exercise I

In the beginning, it might be easier to solve these problems in two or more steps. For example, the problem 2 + 4 - 3 can be solved as 2 + 4 = 6, then 6 - 3 = 3. At some point your child will develop enough automaticity to do both operations simultaneously.

1 + 2 + 2 = 5	4 + 3 - 7 = 0	8 + 5 - 2 - 3 = 8	3 + 7 - 5 = 5
1 + 2 + 3 = 6	2 + 6 - 7 = 1	7 - 4 + 3 = 6	2 + 8 - 7 = 3
2 + 2 + 3 = 7	3 + 5 - 8 = 0	10 - 5 + 2 = 7	4 + 5 - 6 = 3
1 + 2 + 4 = 7	5 + 4 - 8 = 1	6 + 4 - 6 = 4	1 + 5 - 3 = 3
1 + 2 + 5 = 8	5 + 5 - 9 = 1	4 + 4 - 6 = 2	6 - 3 + 2 = 5
1 + 2 + 3 = 6	8 - 3 + 2 = 7	10 - 7 + 4 = 7	7 - 3 + 4 = 8
1 + 2 + 6 = 9	6 + 2 - 4 = 4	10 - 6 + 2 = 6	3 + 5 - 4 = 4
2 + 2 + 1 = 5	7 - 3 + 4 = 8	10 - 4 + 1 = 7	8 - 7 + 6 = 7
2 + 3 + 1 = 6	5 + 5 - 3 = 7	9 - 6 + 3 = 6	5 - 3 + 8 = 10
2 + 3 - 1 = 4	5 - 3 + 6 = 8	9 - 5 + 2 = 6	4 - 2 + 6 = 8
2 + 3 - 5 = 0	8 - 3 + 3 = 8	3 + 5 - 4 = 4	8 - 3 + 5 = 10
4 + 3 + 1 = 8	4 + 3 + 2 - 3 = 6	2 + 7 - 9 = 0	10 - 6 + 4 = 8

Exercise II

10 is made of what number and 5? *Ans:* 5

10 is made of what number and 3? *Ans:* 7

10 is made of what number and 4? *Ans:* 6

10 is made of what number and 8? *Ans:* 2

10 is made of what number and 0? *Ans:* 10

10 is made of what number and 6? *Ans:* 4

10 is made of what number and 9? *Ans:* 1

10 is made of what number and 7? *Ans:* 3

Word Problems

1. Four birds were sitting on a branch. One more bird came and then 2 flew away. How many birds are on the branch?
    Ans: 3 birds (4 + 1 = 5, then 5 - 2 = 3).

2. There were 3 apples in a bowl. I put 2 more in and took out 1. How many apples are in the bowl now? *Ans:* 4 apples (3 + 2 = 5, then 5 - 1 = 4).

3. Four chess players came to the park. Then 2 more players came and 1 player left. How many chess players are in the park now?
    Ans: 5 (4 + 2 = 6, then 6 - 1 = 5).

4. I took 3 steps from the wall. Then I took another 3 steps forward and 2 step backward. How many steps from the wall am I now? *Ans:* 4 steps.

5. Otis had $4 and borrowed $2 more. He spent $2 on lunch. How much money does he have now? *Ans:* $4.

6. I brought 3 tennis balls and Jenny also brought 3 balls. During the game we lost one ball. How many tennis balls do we have now?
    Ans: 5 tennis balls.

7. Mom baked 5 muffins and we ate them all. Then mom baked 5 more and we ate only one. How many muffins are not eaten? *Ans:* 4 muffins.

8. Robert lost his pen. He bought 6 more pens and then found the pen he lost. How many pens does he have now? *Ans:* 7 pens.

9. In the morning, Marisa opened all 6 windows in the house. After breakfast, she closed 3 windows and after lunch she closed another 3. How many windows are open in the house by the dinner time? *Ans:* None.

10. I waited for 3 minutes, then 2 minutes, then another minute. How many minutes did I wait? *Ans:* 6 minutes.

11. A spider caught 2 flies, then 3 flies, then 4 more flies. How many flies did the spider catch altogether? *Ans:* 9 flies.

12. Another spider caught 5 flies and then 3 flies, but 2 flies got away. How many flies are in the spider's web now? *Ans:* 6 flies.

13. Little Tommy counts cars. First, 3 cars passed. Then 2 more cars passed. Then 4 more cars passed. How many cars did he count altogether? *Ans:* 9 cars.

14. During a snowfall, 8 snowflakes fell on my hand. After 6 of them melted, 5 more fell on it. How many snowflakes were on my hand then? *Ans:* 7 snowflakes. Count them quickly before they all melt.

15. A diver collected pearls. She found 9, lost 5, and then found 4 more. How many pearls did she collect? *Ans:* 8 pearls.

16. Alex is making a necklace. He put 3 red beads on a string, then 2 white beads, then 2 blue beads. How many beads did he put on the string altogether? *Ans:* 7 beads.

17. A squirrel hid 2 nuts in the pine tree, 3 nuts in the oak tree, and 4 in the birch tree. How many nuts did the squirrel hide? *Ans:* 9 nuts.

18. There were 9 toys on the floor. I picked up 3 and put them in the basket. Then I picked up another 3 toys, and then 3 more. How many toys are on the floor now? *Ans:* 0 toys.

19. In the Special Olympics, Frank won 2 trophies in baseball, 2 trophies in soccer, and 2 in tennis. How many trophies did he win altogether? *Ans:* 6 trophies.

20. I am the bus driver. At the first stop, 3 people got on the bus. At the second stop, 4 people got on. At the third stop no one got on, but one person stepped off. How many people are on the bus now? *Ans:* 7 people.

    Solution: It's tricky: 3 passengers + 4 passengers - 1 passenger = 6 passengers. But you must include me, the driver. 6 passengers + 1 driver = 7 people.

21. For her birthday, Rebecca received 7 music CDs. She gave 3 to her sister and 2 to her brother. How many CDs did she keep? *Ans:* 2 CDs.

22. There were 8 students in the library. 2 students went to play ball, 2 students went back to class, and 2 students went home. How many students are still in the library? *Ans:* 2 students.

23. There are 8 players on my team. 4 players are boys. How many girls are on the team? *Ans:* 4 girls.

24. There are 8 players on my soccer team. 1 goalie, 2 defense, 2 midfielders, and the rest are forwards. How many forwards are on my team? *Ans:* 3 forwards.

25. Today, 4 groups of students came to the museum. Later 4 more groups of students came. At noon, 3 groups left. How many groups are still in the museum? *Ans:* 5 groups.

26. Three pears, 3 apples, and 2 oranges are in the fruit bowl. I ate all 3 apples. How many fruits are in the bowl now? *Ans:* 5 fruits.

27. Cory had 6 baby teeth. He grew 3 more baby teeth. Two years later, 4 of his baby teeth fell out. How many teeth does Cory have now? *Ans:* 5 teeth.

28. There were 7 large pictures on the wall. Kim took 3 large pictures off the wall and hung 5 small pictures instead. How many pictures, large and small, are on the wall now? *Ans:* 9 pictures.

29. Ten people are working at a carwash, 3 are washing a car, 4 are washing a truck. How many people are waiting for the next customer? *Ans:* 3 people.

30. Uma loves ringing doorbells. At her aunt's house she rang the doorbell 6 times, then 3 times more, and then 1 more time before her mother told her to stop. How many times did Uma ring the doorbell? *Ans:* 10 times.

31. Uma's aunt has an old dog who barks when he hears the doorbell ring. The dog barked once, then 3 more times, then 4 times more. How many times did the dog bark?
    Ans: 8 times. The dog is old and missed some doorbells.

32. Uma's aunt also has a cat that meows when the dog barks. The cat meowed 4 times, then 3 more times, then 3 times again. How many times did the cat meow?
    Ans: 10. Cat likes to meow.

33. There is a mouse that lives under Uma's aunt's house. This mouse squeaks when the cat meows. The mouse squeaked 4 times, then 2 more, and then 2 more times. How many times did the mouse squeak?
    Ans: 8. It was so loud that no one heard the little mouse.

34. Garth had 5 baseball cards. He traded away 4 and received back 6. How many cards does he have now? *Ans:* 7 cards.

35. Guy had 5 melons. Paul had 4 more than Guy. How many melons did Paul have? *Ans:* 9 melons.

36. Paul was carrying 6 melons. He dropped and broke 3 melons, how many does he have now? *Ans:* 3 melons.

37. Fred noticed 7 flies on the windowsill and shooed them away. Only 5 flies flew away but 7 new flies came. How many flies are sitting on the windowsill now? *Ans:* 9 flies.

38. Pam had 9 buttons. She gave away 6 and bought 5 more. How many buttons does she have now? *Ans:* 8 buttons.

39. A glass had 8 ounces of water. I drank 4 ounces and then poured in 3 more. How many ounces of water are in the glass now? *Ans:* 7 ounces.

40. There were 9 flowers in a vase. I took out 7 flowers and put in 6 new ones. How many flowers are in the vase now? *Ans:* 8 flowers.

41. Next day, I added 2 new flowers and took out 3 old ones. How many flowers are in the vase now? *Ans:* 7 flowers.

42. There are 7 peas on my plate. I ate 6 but mom put 5 more. How many peas are on my plate now? *Ans:* 6 peas.

43. Then mom put 3 more and I ate 5. How many peas are on the plate? *Ans:* 4 peas.

44. Then mom put 5 more and I ate 8. How many peas are on the plate? *Ans:* 1 pea.

45. For the bonfire, the scouts brought 4 small sticks, 3 medium size sticks and 1 large stick. How many sticks are there for the bonfire? *Ans:* 8 sticks.

46. Karim had 5 dollars. He borrowed $3 more, but spent only $2. How much money does he have now? *Ans:* $6.

47. I have 3 pencils, Jack has 3 pencils, and Carlos has 3 pencils. How many pencils do we have altogether? *Ans:* 9 pencils.

48. There were 10 crayons in a box. I took out 8 to draw a picture, but 1 crayon broke. I put back the rest. How many crayons are in the box now? *Ans:* 9 crayons.

49. There were 10 pigeons in the square. Seven pigeons flew away and 6 came back. How many pigeons are there now? *Ans:* 9 pigeons.
    a) Then 6 pigeons flew away and 5 came back. How many pigeons are there now? *Ans:* 8 pigeons.
    b) Now, there are 8 pigeons. If 6 pigeons fly away and 4 come back, how many pigeons will be in the square? *Ans:* 6 pigeons.

50. There were 8 cars in the garage. In the morning 7 cars left and 6 cars came in. How many cars are there now? *Ans:* 7 cars.
    a) In the afternoon 5 cars left and 3 cars came. How many cars are in the garage? *Ans:* 5 cars.
    b) In the evening 4 cars left and 5 cars came. How many cars are in the garage? *Ans:* 6 cars.

51. Take number 5. Take away 3 and add 5. Then take away 4 and add 5. Then take away 6 and add 5. What's the new number?
    Ans: 7 (5 - 3 + 5 = 7, then 7 - 4 + 5 = 8, then 8 - 6 + 5 = 7).

52. Take an 8 inch red ribbon and cut 3 inches off. Then take a 7 inch white ribbon and cut 2 inches off. Now sew the remaining pieces together. How long is the new ribbon? *Ans:* 10 inches (8 - 3 = 5, 7 - 2 = 5, 5 + 5 = 10).

53. There were 3 apples and 4 oranges in the fruit basket. James took 1 apple and 2 oranges. How many apples and oranges are left in the basket?

Solution: Let me show you 2 ways to solve this problem.
One way: There were 3 apples and James took 1, that is 3 - 1 = 2, 2 apples are left.   There were 4 oranges and James took 2, that is 4 - 2 = 2, 2 oranges are left.
2 apples and 2 oranges make 4. The answer is 4.
Another way: There were 3 apples and 4 oranges. Together that makes 7 fruits.
James took 1 apple, that is 7 - 1 = 6. He also took 2 oranges, 6 - 2 = 4. The answer is 4.

A challenge
54. Take number 9. Add 1 and take away 2. Then add 1 to the new number and take away 2 again. Keep doing it with each new number. How many times do you have to add 1 and take away 2 until you reach 0?
Ans: 9 times.

Exercises with 10

Exercise I

What do you add to 9 to make 10?	*Ans:* 1
What do you add to 1 to make 10?	*Ans:* 9
What do you add to 4 to make 10?	*Ans:* 6
What do you add to 10 to make 10?	*Ans:* 0
What do you add to 3 to make 10?	*Ans:* 7
What do you add to 8 to make 10?	*Ans:* 2
What do you add to 5 to make 10?	*Ans:* 5
What do you add to 6 to make 10?	*Ans:* 4
What do you add to 2 to make 10?	*Ans:* 8
What do you add to 3 to make 10?	*Ans:* 7

Exercise II

1 + 9 = 10	10 - 2 = 8	5 + 8 + 2 = 15	9 - 4 = 5	9 + 1 - 2 = 8
2 + 8 = 10	10 - 8 = 2	2 + 8 + 3 = 13	9 - 5 = 4	8 + 2 - 1 = 9
3 + 7 = 10	10 - 0 = 10	4 + 4 + 5 = 13	9 - 6 = 3	8 + 2 - 3 = 7
4 + 5 = 9	10 - 4 = 6	10 - 4 - 4 = 2	9 - 7 = 2	7 + 1 - 2 = 6
5 + 5 = 10	10 - 6 = 4	8 - 2 = 6	7 - 4 = 3	6 + 4 - 5 = 5
6 + 4 = 10	10 - 7 = 3	8 - 3 = 5	7 - 3 = 4	5 + 5 - 2 = 8
7 + 2 = 9	3 + 7 = 10	8 - 4 = 4	7 - 2 = 5	4 + 4 + 2 = 10
6 + 3 = 9	3 + 3 + 7 = 13	8 - 5 = 3	7 - 5 = 2	3 + 1 - 2 = 2
5 + 5 = 10	4 + 7 + 3 = 14	8 - 6 = 2	5 - 3 = 2	10 - 2 - 2 - 2 = 4
1 + 9 = 10	8 + 4 + 1 = 13	9 - 2 = 7	7 + 7 = 14	10 - 3 - 3 - 3 = 1
2 + 8 = 10	7 + 5 + 3 = 15	9 - 3 = 6	6 + 4 = 10	1 + 1 - 2 = 0

Word Problems

1. I have 4 buttons in my left pocket and 4 buttons in my right pocket. How many more buttons do I need to make 10? *Ans:* 2 buttons.

   Solution: 4 (buttons in the left pocket) + 4 (buttons in the right pocket) = 8 (buttons in both pockets). Then, 10 buttons - 8 buttons = 2 buttons.

2. Out of 10 chairs around the table, 5 are taken. How many are free?
    Ans: 5 chairs.

3. Ten apples were on the table, now there are only 4. How many are gone?
    Ans: 6 apples.

4. Grace had 10 stamps and put 7 on the envelope. How many stamps are left? *Ans:* 3 stamps.

5. Doris had 6 kittens and brought home 3 more. Does she have 10 kittens now? *Ans:* No, she has only 9 kittens.

6. Today is my birthday, I am 5. Mom bought 10 birthday candles to put on my cake. Will we have enough candles left for my next birthday too? *Ans:* No. I'll be 6 next year and there are only 5 candles left.

7. Together my brother and I had 10 dollars. My brother took $5 without telling me. Did he leave me my fair share? *Ans:* Yes, he left me half, $5.

8. Anna has 3 marbles and I have 4. How many do we need to make 10? *Ans:* 3 marbles.

9. Pedro bought 5 tomatoes and he has 3 at home. How many more does he need to make 10? *Ans:* 2 more tomatoes.

10. Heather had 10 plums. She gave 2 to Albert, 3 to Boris, and 5 to Candice. How many plums she kept for herself? *Ans:* 0 plums.

11. Margo took 10 peanuts for squirrels. She gave 3 peanuts to the first squirrel, 3 to the next, and 3 more to the third. How many peanuts does she have for the 4th squirrel? *Ans:* 1 peanut.

12. Jamie has to deliver 10 flyers. She already delivered 3. How many does she still have with her? *Ans:* 7 flyers.

13. Jill is cutting her toenails. She cut 4 nails on the right side and 4 nails on the left. How many more toenails does she have to cut? *Ans:* 2 more toenails.

14. Asha has a 10 day vacation. She plans to spend 3 days at her grandmother's house, 3 days at her aunt's house and 2 days at her friend's house. How many days will she have left before school starts? *Ans:* 2 days.

    Solution: 3 days + 3 days + 2 days = 8 days.
    Then 10 days (vacation) - 8 days = 2 days.

15. A delivery truck carried 10 boxes. It delivered 4 boxes at the first stop, then 2 boxes at the second stop, then 3 boxes at the third stop. He was tired so he parked under a tree and took a nap. While he was sleeping, thieves stole 1 box. How many boxes are left on the truck? *Ans:* 0 boxes.

16. Pretend you are a bus driver. At the first stop 5 passengers came in. At the next stop 5 more passengers got on and 3 left, then 2 students got on and 4 left the bus, then no one got on and 4 passengers left the bus, then an old lady got on with a cat, and then everyone left. How old is the bus driver? *Ans:* Tricky! Remember, you are the driver. How old are you?

17. There were 10 kittens in a shelter. The first family took home 2 kittens, another family took 2 more. Then a lady took 2 more kittens. How many kittens are still in the shelter? *Ans:* 4 kittens (10 - 2 - 2 - 2 = 4).

18. Forrest had 10 golf balls. The first day of playing, he lost 3 balls. The second day, he lost another 3 golf balls. How many golf balls does he have left? *Ans:* 4 golfballs.

19. Rocky will need $10 to buy a present for his sister. If he has $3, how much more would he need? *Ans:* $7.
    a) If he has $5, how much would he need? *Ans:* $5.
    b) If he saved $6, how much more does he have to find? *Ans:* $4.

20. Olivia signed up for 10 guitar lessons. She had 4 lessons last month and 4 lessons this month. How many more lessons are left? *Ans:* 2 lessons.

21. Drew shot 10 arrows. Only 3 hit the target. How many arrows missed? *Ans:* 7 arrows.

22. Sparky, a poodle, received 10 treats for his 10th birthday. There were 3 turkey, 3 lamb and 3 veggie treats. The rest were fish. How many fish treats did Sparky get? *Ans:* 1 fish treat.

23 Ida needs 10 awards to win a competition. She received 4 awards in swimming and 3 awards for diving. How many more does she need to win? *Ans:* 3 more awards.

24. Leo has to return 10 books to the library. He found 2 books on the sofa, 3 under his bed and 3 more in the closet. How many books are missing? *Ans:* 2 books.

25. Ten ducks were sitting on the beach. Then 2 ducks jumped in the water, then 3 more jumped in the water, then 2 flew away. How many ducks are now on the beach? *Ans:* 3 ducks.

26. Hold out both hands. Bend your fingers.
    a) Bend 3 fingers and tell me how many fingers are not bent? *Ans:* 7 fingers.
    b) Bend 5 fingers and tell me how many fingers are not bent? *Ans:* 5 fingers.
    c) Bend 6 fingers and tell me how many fingers are not bent? *Ans:* 4 fingers.
    d) Bend 10 fingers and tell me how many fingers are not bent? *Ans:* 0 fingers.

27. There are 10 digits in a telephone number and Glenn forgot 2. How many digits did he remember? *Ans*: 8 digits.

28. Out of a toolbox of 10 screwdrivers, 3 are being used for a project and 2 are missing. How many are in the box? *Ans*: 5 screwdrivers.

29. Out of the 10 songs Ingrid knows, 3 are country, 3 are hip-hop, 3 are blues and the rest are oldies. How many oldies songs does Ingrid know? *Ans:* 1 oldie. It might be a Beatles song, but I am not sure.

30. Out of 10 postcards, Kurt sent to his pen pals, 2 came back because of wrong addresses and 3 came back because they didn't have a stamp. How many reached his pen pals? *Ans*: 5 postcards.

32. There were 10 ten boxes of cereal on the shelf in the morning. By the end of the day there were six boxes left. How many boxes were sold? *Ans*: 4 boxes.

33. Olivia signed up for singing lessons. She had 10 lessons last month and 10 lessons this month. How many lessons has she taken so far? *Ans*: 20 lessons.

34. Robin Hood shot 10 practice arrows. Only 5 hit the target. How many arrows missed? *Ans*: 5 arrows.

35. Tamme moved to our street when she was 5 years old. She is ten years old now. How many years has she been living on our street? *Ans*: 5 years.

36. Drew is 10 years old. How old was he 4 years ago? *Ans*: 6 years old.

Addition up to 12

Problem Solving

First Problem: what is 9 + 2?

Solution: Step 1: 2 equals to 1 + 1,
Step 2: We can say then that 9 + 2 is the same as 9 + 1 + 1.
Step 3: 9 + 1 = 10, 10 + 1 = 11
The answer: 9 + 2 = 11.

↪ *The rule: Adding any number to 9*
To add any number to 9, you will need to take away 1 from the number and then add what is left to 10.

Second Problem: what is 7 + 5 = ?

Solution: Step 1: To solve this problem we split the number 5 into two parts, 3 and 2, because 3 and 2 make 5.
Step 2: Then we can say that 7 + 5 is the same as 7 + 3 and then adding 2.
Step 3: 7 + 3 = 10, 10 + 2 = 12
The answer: 7 + 5 = 12.

Let's solve the second problem a different way: 5 + 7 = ?

Solution: Step 1: This time we will split the number 7 into two parts, 5 and 2.
Step 2: Then we can say that 7 + 5 is the same as 5 + 5 + 2.
Step 3: 5 + 5 = 10, you know that, therefore 10 + 2 = 12.
The answer: 7 + 5 = 12.

Exercise I

4 + 4 = 8	2 + 10 = 12	3 + 6 = 9	4 + 3 = 7	4 + 4 = 8
4 + 5 = 9	3 + 1 = 4	3 + 7 = 10	4 + 4 = 8	5 + 3 = 8
3 + 3 = 6	3 - 1 = 2	3 + 8 = 11	4 + 5 = 9	5 + 4 = 9
3 + 4 = 7	3 + 2 = 5	3 + 9 = 12	9 - 5 = 4	5 + 5 = 10
7 - 3 = 4	8 - 3 = 5	6 - 3 = 3	4 + 6 = 10	5 + 6 = 11
2 + 5 = 7	3 + 3 = 6	6 + 3 = 9	4 + 7 = 11	6 + 6 = 12
2 + 6 = 8	3 + 4 = 7	6 + 6 = 12	4 + 8 = 12	5 + 7 = 12
2 + 8 = 10	3 + 5 = 8	3 + 3 = 6	8 - 4 = 4	7 + 5 = 12
2 + 9 = 11	8 - 4 = 4	6 - 2 = 4	5 + 2 = 7	6 + 6 = 12

6 + 5 = 11	7 + 3 = 10	10 - 6 = 4	10 - 8 = 2	3 + 8 = 11
9 + 3 = 12	7 + 4 = 11	8 + 2 = 10	9 + 1 = 10	6 + 6 = 12
7 + 5 = 12	7 + 2 = 9	8 + 3 = 11	10 + 1 = 11	4 + 7 = 11
5 + 6 = 11	7 + 5 = 12	8 + 4 = 12	9 + 2 = 11	10 - 7 = 3
7 + 1 = 8	7 - 4 = 3	8 + 2 = 10	9 + 3 = 12	5 + 6 + 1 = 12

Exercise II

7 is made of 6 and what number?	*Ans:* 1
7 is made of 5 and what number?	*Ans:* 2
8 is made of 7 and what number?	*Ans:* 1
8 is made of 8 and what number?	*Ans:* 0
8 is made of 5 and what number?	*Ans:* 3
10 is made of 5 and what number?	*Ans:* 5
7 is made of 3 and what number?	*Ans:* 4
9 is made of 8 and what number?	*Ans:* 1
9 is made of 7 and what number?	*Ans:* 2
7 is made of 4 and what number?	*Ans:* 3
10 is made of 9 and what number?	*Ans:* 1
6 is made of 2 and what number?	*Ans:* 4
11 is made of 8 and what number?	*Ans:* 3
7 is made of 1 and what number?	*Ans:* 6
8 is made of 1 and what number?	*Ans:* 7
12 is made of 6 and what number?	*Ans:* 6
10 is made of 5 and what number?	*Ans:* 5
11 is made of 10 and what number?	*Ans:* 1
10 is made of 3 and what number?	*Ans:* 7

Exercise III

5 + 4 = 9	2 + 9 = 11	5 + 6 = 11	3 + 7 = 10	5 + 5 = 10
6 + 3 = 9	9 + 2 = 11	5 + 4 = 9	5 + 7 = 12	4 + 4 = 8
3 + 6 = 9	4 + 8 = 12	5 + 7 = 12	6 + 5 = 11	3 + 4 = 7
7 + 2 = 9	8 + 4 = 12	8 + 3 = 11	2 + 9 = 11	4 + 5 = 9
5 + 5 = 10	6 + 3 = 9	8 + 4 = 12	4 + 7 = 11	5 + 3 = 8
6 + 5 = 11	3 + 9 = 12	3 + 8 = 11	3 + 9 = 12	2 + 3 = 5
6 + 6 = 12	7 + 5 = 12	4 + 6 = 10	6 + 6 = 12	5 + 1 = 6

Word Problems

1. I picked up 10 magazines from behind the desk. Then I picked up 1 more from the chair. How many magazines did I pick up altogether? *Ans:* 11 magazines.

2. If I had 6 lizards and then I caught 5 more, how many lizards do I have now? *Ans:* 11 lizards.

3. We planted 10 bushes. Then we planted 2 more. How many bushes did we plant? *Ans:* 12 bushes.

4. My right shoe has 6 holes for a shoelace. My left shoe also has 6. How many holes are on both shoes? *Ans:* 12 holes.

5. I solved 7 problems and Gwen solved another 4. How many did we solve together? *Ans:* 11 problems.

6. There were 8 balls on a pool table before Kwesi shot 4 balls in the pockets. How many balls are on the table now? *Ans:* 4 balls.

7. I invited 9 friends to my party. They brought 3 of their friends. How many kids came? *Ans:* 12 kids.

8. I used 7 long wires and 4 short wires for a project. How many wires did I use altogether? *Ans:* 11 wires.

9. I packed 3 oatmeal cookies, 4 chocolate chip cookies and 4 peanut cookies. How many cookies did I pack? *Ans:* 11 cookies (3 + 4 = 7, 7 + 4 = 11).

10. I bought 6 new books and put them on the shelf. If there are 6 books on the shelf already, how many books are on the shelf now? *Ans:* 12 books.

11. I am 9 years old. How old will I be in 3 years? *Ans:* 12 years old.

12. Bjorn is 7 years old. How old will he be in 4 years? *Ans:* 11 years old.

13. You are 6 years old. How old will you be in 5 years? *Ans:* 11 years old.

14. My sister is 7 years old. How old will she be in 5 years? *Ans:* 12 years old.

15. My dog is 5 years old. How old will it be in 6 years? *Ans:* 11 years old.

16. Today, Jack came over and stayed for 5 hours. Then he left but came right back and stayed for another 5 hours. How many hours did he stay at our house in total? *Ans:* 10 hours.

17. A police officer stopped 10 drivers and gave tickets to 2 drivers. How many drivers didn't get tickets? *Ans:* 8 drivers.

18. I have 6 freckles on my right cheek and 6 on the other. How many freckles do I have? *Ans:* 12 freckles.

19. On a skyscraper sat 4 crows. 7 more crows came and sat next to them. How many crows are sitting on the skyscraper now? *Ans:* 11 crows.

20. Cory sniffled 6 times. Then he blew his nose and sniffled 5 more times. How many times did he sniffle altogether? *Ans:* 11 times.

21. I had $5 and my aunt gave me $6 more. How much money do I have now? *Ans:* $11.

22. A girl paid 4 cents for bubble gum, 3 cents for a balloon and 5 cents for a plastic ring. How much money did she spend? *Ans:* 12 cents.

23. If you drew 3 red, 4 green and 6 yellow circles, how many circles did you draw? *Ans:* More than 12.

24. If 4 letters came on Monday, 3 on Tuesday, 2 on Wednesday, 3 on Thursday and none for rest of the week, how many letters came that week? *Ans:* 12 letters (4 + 3 + 2 + 3 + 0 = 12).

25. If a door bell rang 5 times and then 3 times and then 3 more times, how many times did it ring? *Ans:* 11 times.

26. I gave my dog 4 treats. He wanted more, so I gave him 6 more. My mom told me not to give my dog more than 10 treats in a day. Did I go over the limit? *Ans:* No (4 + 6 = 10).

27. At my party, there were 3 boys and 8 girls. How many children came to my party? *Ans:* 11 children.

28. Six birds of feather flocked together with 5 birds without feathers. How many birds, with and without feathers, flocked together? *Ans:* 11 birds.

29. For a costume parade, 4 kids came dressed like dragons, 5 as monsters, and 1 in a bunny suit. How many kids came for the parade? *Ans:* 10 children.

30. Ava counted 4 yellow cars and 7 red cars on the road. How many cars did she count? *Ans:* 11 cars.

31. My grandma has 8 pairs of eye glasses and 3 pairs of sunglasses. How many pairs of glasses does she have? *Ans:* 11 pairs of glasses.

32. Lin bought 8 bagels; four of them had poppy seeds. How many were of the other kind? *Ans:* 4 bagels.

33. While holding 4 birds in his hands, Mr. Porter noticed 8 birds in the bush. How many birds were there in the hands and in the bush? *Ans:* 12 birds.

34. Six toads invited 6 frogs for a singing party at midnight. How many amphibians (toads and frogs) were at the party? *Ans:* 12 amphibians.

35. Mila baked 4 square cookies, 4 triangular and 4 round cookies. How many cookies did she bake? *Ans:* 12 cookies.

36. A jacket has 6 buttons on the right and 6 on the left. How many buttons are there? *Ans:* 12 buttons.

37. A class has 9 children everyday. One day, 4 children got flu and didn't come to school. How many children are in class today? *Ans:* 5 children.

38. Neal had 3 spoonfuls of chicken soup and then had 8 more. How many spoonfuls did he have? *Ans:* 11 spoons of chicken soup. They say chicken soup is good for you when you have the flu.

39. A woman washed 6 silk handkerchiefs and 5 handkerchiefs made of cotton. How many handkerchiefs did she wash in total? *Ans:* 11 handkerchiefs.

40. A senator had 5 visitors from China and 4 from Japan. How many visitors did she have? *Ans:* 9 visitors.

41. A lady has 6 summer hats and 6 winter hats. How many hats does she have? *Ans:* 12 hats.

42. A boxer has 5 right gloves and 5 left gloves. How many gloves does he have? *Ans:* 10 gloves.

43. A poor man has 4 holes in his right pocket and 8 in the left pocket. How many holes does he have in both? *Ans:* 12 holes.

44. My neighbor on the right has 5 goats and the other one on the left has 7. How many goats do they both have? *Ans:* 12 goats.

45. One company has 3 tow trucks, another has 9. How many trucks do both have? *Ans:* 12 trucks.

46. I counted 6 ladybugs on 5 bushes and Mia found 6 ladybugs on 4 bushes. How many bushes did we check for ladybugs? *Ans:* 9 bushes. Always pay attention to the question.

47. My brother caught a fish weighing 2 pounds and I caught a 7-pound fish. How much do both fish weigh? *Ans:* 9 lbs.

48. For their birthdays, twins received 6 music CDs each. How many music CDs did they both get? *Ans:* 12 CDs.

Lesson 12

Addition up to 15

Problem Solving

Problem: 9 + 5 = ?
Solution: Step 1: the number 5 is made of 1 and 4 (because 1 + 4 = 5)
              Step 2: then 9 + 1 = 10, and then 10 + 4 = 14
              The answer: 9 + 5 = 14.

Problem: 2 + 12 = ?
Solution: Step 1: 2 + 12 is the same as 12 + 2 and that equals 14
              The answer: 2 + 12 = 14.

Problem: 6 + 7 = ?
Solution: Step 1: 7 is made of 4 and 3 (because 4 + 3 = 7)
              Step 2: then 6 + 4 = 10, and then 10 + 3 = 13
              The answer: 6 + 7 = 13.

Exercise I

5 + 2 = 7	6 + 4 = 10	7 + 8 = 15	9 + 2 = 11	9 + 4 = 13
5 + 3 = 8	6 + 5 = 11	8 + 6 = 14	10 + 3 = 13	9 + 6 = 15
5 + 4 = 9	6 + 7 = 13	9 + 2 = 11	7 + 6 = 13	8 + 7 = 15
5 + 5 = 10	6 + 6 = 12	9 + 3 = 12	8 + 4 = 12	9 + 5 = 14
5 + 6 = 11	6 + 8 = 14	9 + 4 = 13	4 + 9 = 13	5 + 8 = 13
5 + 7 = 12	6 + 9 = 15	8 + 5 = 13	5 + 8 = 13	5 + 6 = 11
5 + 8 = 13	7 + 4 = 11	9 + 5 = 14	6 + 8 = 14	5 + 7 = 12
5 + 9 = 14	7 + 5 = 12	9 + 6 = 15	7 + 6 = 13	4 + 7 = 11
5 + 10 = 15	7 + 7 = 14	8 + 7 = 15	7 + 7 = 14	6 + 6 = 12

Exercise II

How much do you add to 9 to make 13?   *Ans:* 4
How much do you add to 3 to make 13?   *Ans:* 10
How much do you add to 5 to make 13?   *Ans:* 8
How much do you add to 6 to make 13?   *Ans:* 7
How much do you add to 14 to make 15?   *Ans:* 1
How much do you add to 12 to make 15?   *Ans:* 3
How much do you add to 10 to make 15?   *Ans:* 5

How much do you add to 15 to make 15?   *Ans:* 0
How much do you add to 11 to make 15?   *Ans:* 4
How much do you add to 9 to make 15?   *Ans:* 6
How much do you add to 5 to make 15?   *Ans:* 10
How much do you add to 4 to make 15?   *Ans:* 11
How much do you add to 7 to make 15?   *Ans:* 8
How much do you add to 8 to make 15?   *Ans:* 7
How much do you add to 6 to make 15?   *Ans:* 9
How much do you add to 3 to make 15?   *Ans:* 12
How much do you add to 1 to make 15?   *Ans:* 14
How much do you add to 2 to make 15?   *Ans:* 13
How much do you add to 7 to make 14?   *Ans:* 7
How much do you add to 6 to make 14?   *Ans:* 8
How much do you add to 8 to make 13?   *Ans:* 5

Exercise III

$8 + 2 + 2 = 12$	$4 + 4 + 2 + 1 = 11$	$12 + 1 = 13$	$4 + 5 + 6 = 15$
$8 + 4 = 12$	$10 + 1 = 11$	$10 + 2 = 12$	$8 + 3 + 2 = 13$
$8 + 2 + 3 = 13$	$9 + 3 + 2 = 14$	$2 + 9 = 11$	$7 + 7 + 1 = 15$
$8 + 5 = 13$	$7 + 4 + 4 = 15$	$8 + 2 = 10$	$7 + 4 + 4 = 15$
$8 + 7 = 15$	$6 + 5 + 3 = 14$	$6 + 7 = 13$	$4 + 4 + 4 = 12$
$8 + 2 + 4 = 14$	$9 + 2 + 2 = 13$	$7 + 6 = 13$	$3 + 3 + 3 + 3 = 12$
$8 + 6 = 14$	$6 + 1 + 7 = 14$	$7 + 7 = 14$	$4 + 3 + 4 + 3 = 14$
$7 + 3 + 1 = 11$	$7 + 2 + 5 = 14$	$3 + 9 = 12$	$3 + 2 + 6 = 11$
$7 + 3 + 4 = 14$	$9 + 2 + 3 = 14$	$5 + 6 = 11$	$5 + 2 + 5 = 12$
$8 + 2 + 5 = 15$	$4 + 8 + 3 = 15$	$7 + 6 = 13$	$5 + 2 + 3 + 4 = 14$
$6 + 4 + 4 + 14$	$5 + 3 + 6 = 14$	$9 + 4 = 13$	$3 + 6 + 4 + 1 = 14$
$5 + 5 + 5 = 15$	$5 + 3 + 2 = 10$	$9 + 5 = 14$	$3 + 5 + 7 = 15$
$7 + 3 + 3 = 13$	$4 + 7 + 2 = 13$	$5 + 9 = 14$	$2 + 3 + 4 + 5 = 14$
$4 + 6 + 4 = 14$	$3 + 6 + 4 = 13$	$5 + 8 = 13$	$5 + 5 + 2 = 12$
$3 + 7 + 2 = 12$	$11 + 1 = 12$	$6 + 4 + 4 = 14$	$5 + 4 + 5 = 14$

Word Problems

1. Ella paid 5 cents for a pencil and 9 cents for an eraser. How much did she pay for both? *Ans:* 14 cents.

2. There are 7 pears on one branch and 6 on another. How many are on both branches? *Ans:* 13 pears.

3. Alice has 5 apples, and her brother has 5. How many apples they both have? *Ans:* 10 apples.

4. Elmo picked up 8 bags, and I picked up 4. How many bags did we pick up together? *Ans:* 12 bags.

5. A farmer planted 7 acres of land with potatoes and 8 acres with corn. How many acres were planted? *Ans:* 15 acres.

6. Anna made 7 pies, and Kate made 4. How many pies did they both make? *Ans:* 11 pies.

7. There are 8 regular chairs in the room and 4 armchairs. How many are there of both kinds? *Ans:* 12 chairs.

8. There are 11 cars on one lot and 4 on another. How many cars are on both? *Ans:* 15 cars.

9. Diana is 9 years old.
    a) How old she will be in 2 years? *Ans:* 11 years old.
    b) In 3 years? *Ans:* 12 years old.
    c) In 5 years? *Ans:* 14 years old.
    d) In 6 years? *Ans:* 15 years old.

10. Jasper had 6 flashlights, and he bought 8 more. How many are there now? *Ans:* 14 flashlights.

11. If a box of pencils costs $6, and a notebook costs $5, what do they both cost? *Ans:* $11.

12. Frank caught 5 fish, and Samuel caught 7. How many did they both catch? *Ans:* 12 fish.

13. Jennie picked 8 pebbles, and Clara picked 5. How many did they both pick? *Ans:* 13 pebbles.

14. There are 5 students in one class and 9 in another. How many students are in both classes? *Ans:* 14 students.

15. If there are 5 letters in my first name and 10 in my last name, how many letters are in my full name? *Ans:* 15 letters. How many letters are in your name?

16. There are 2 boxes on the floor. Each box has 6 toys. How many toys are in both? *Ans:* 12 toys.

17. A farmer sold 8 sacks of coffee last week and 6 sacks today. How many sacks did he sell? *Ans:* 14 sacks.

18. Krista bought 6 birthday cards and 9 "Thank You" cards. How many cards did she buy? *Ans:* 15 cards.

19. In a class there are 7 boys and 7 girls. How many students are in the class? *Ans:* 14 students.

20. There are 7 sparrows in one tree and 8 in another. How many are on both? *Ans:* 15 sparrows.

21. A T-shirt cost $6 and a pair of shorts $7. How much did they both cost? *Ans:* $13.

22. I planted 5 mango trees and 7 guava trees. How many trees did I plant? *Ans:* 12 trees.

23. Robert worked 5 days in one store and 9 days in another. How many days did he work? *Ans:* 14 days.

24. There are 2 pencil holders on the desk. Each has 7 pencils. How many pencils are in both? *Ans:* 14 pencils.

25. The coach made 8 phone calls in the morning and 5 calls after lunch. How many phone calls did she make? *Ans:* 13 calls.

26. Rose picked 5 irises and Iris picked 7 roses. How many flowers did they both pick? *Ans:* 12 flowers.

27. Robin saw 8 jays and Jay saw 6 robins. How many birds did they both see? *Ans:* 14 birds.

28. I saw 8 starfish in the fish tank and also 5 shrimp. How many sea creatures did I see? *Ans:* 13 sea creatures.

29. In a room, there are 7 lamps that are turned on and 7 lamps that are off. How many lamps are in the room? *Ans:* 14 lamps.

30. In the pool, Phoebe made 6 cannonballs, 3 nose dives and 4 belly flops. How many dives did Phoebe make altogether? *Ans:* 13 dives.

31. In the toolbox, June found 8 screwdrivers, 3 pliers and 1 hammer. How many tools are in the box? *Ans:* 12 tools.

32. While cleaning the schoolyard, David found 5 wrappers, 5 empty cans and 4 used napkins. How many items did David find? *Ans:* 14 items.

33. Last month an inventor had 5 new ideas. This month she had another 8. How many ideas did she have? *Ans:* 13 ideas.

34. The radio played 9 old songs and 6 new ones. How many songs did it play? *Ans:* 15 songs.

35. At first, 3 students left the room, then 4 students, then 5 more were gone. How many students left the room? *Ans:* 12 students.

36. For the salad, Matt took 4 carrots, 5 tomatoes and 6 cucumbers. How many veggies did Matt use altogether? *Ans:* 15 veggies.

37. Billy, the joker, rang the neighbor's doorbell with 8 short rings and 7 long ones. As a punishment he wrote "I am sorry" for each ring. How many times did Billy write "I am sorry"?
    Ans: 15 times. That will teach him a lesson.

38. The father can chop 8 pieces of wood in 10 minutes, and the son can chop 4 in 10 minutes. How many pieces can they both chop in 10 minutes?
    Ans: 12 pieces.

39. A wire was cut into 2 pieces. One piece is 8 feet long and the other is 7 feet. How long was the wire before they cut it? *Ans:* 15 feet.

40. A movie editor will cut 6 hours from an 8 hour long movie. How many hours of the movie he will keep? *Ans:* 2 hours.

41. A store owner sold 6 bags of flour to one person, and 7 bags to another. How many bags did he sell? *Ans:* 13 bags.

42. Fred owns 9 ducks, and his brother owns 5. How many ducks do they both have? *Ans:* 14 ducks.

43. If it takes 9 hours to drive from my town to New York City, and then another 5 hours to Boston. How many hours does it take to drive from my town to Boston? *Ans:* 14 hours.

44. A library received 4 sports magazines, 5 fashion magazines and 4 travel magazines. How many magazines did the library receive?
    Ans: 13 magazines.

45. An architect drew a house with 4 windows on the left side, 4 windows on the right, 4 windows in front and 2 in the back. How many windows does the house have? *Ans:* 14 windows (4 + 4 + 4 + 2 = 14).

46. From the garden patch, Mervin picked 3 tomatoes, 3 potatoes, 3 carrots and 3 cucumbers. How many vegetables did he pick altogether?
    Ans: 12 vegetables.

47. My dad is 6 feet tall, my sister is 5 feet. How tall will they be if my sister stands on top of my dad? *Ans:* 11 feet. Though it will look silly.

48. Camille borrowed 11 books from the library and returned 4. How many books does she have now? *Ans:* 7 books.

49. In the chess competition Gina won 6 games, lost 6 games, and 3 games ended with a draw. How many games did she play altogether?
    Ans: 15 games.

50. In one day, a tourist saw 4 museums, 4 shows, 4 parks and 1 fort. How many places did she visit? *Ans:* 13 places.

51. A wire was cut into 2 pieces. One piece is 6 feet long and the other is 5 feet. How long was the wire before they cut it? *Ans:* 11 feet.

52. A newspaper editor will cut an article from 11 columns to 8 columns long.How many columns did he cut? *Ans:* 3 columns.

53. A florist sold 6 bouquets to one person, and 7 bouquets to another. How many bouquets did she sell? *Ans:* 13 bouquets.

Subtraction with numbers up to 15

Exercise I

Count backward from 15 by 1 (i.e., 15, 14, 13, etc.)
Count backward from 15 by 2 (i.e., 15, 13, 11, 9, etc.)
Count backward from 15 by 3 (i.e., 15, 12, 9, 6, 3, 0)
Count backward from 15 by 4 (i.e., 15, 11, 7, 3)
Count backward from 15 by 5 (i.e., 15, 10, 5, 0)
Count backward from 15 by 6 (i.e., 15, 9, 3)
Count backward from 15 by 7 (i.e., 15, 8, 1)

Problem Solving

First problem: What is 12 - 3 = ?
Solution: Step 1: the number 3 is made of 2 and 1
Step 2: then 12 - 3 can be solved by first 12 - 2 and then take away 1. 12 - 2 = 10, then 10 - 1 = 9
The answer: 12 - 3 = 9.

Second problem: What is 13 - 8 = ?
Solution: Step 1: 8 can be broken into 3 and 5.
Step 2: Now, 13 - 8 can be solved as 13 - 3 and then take away 5. 13 - 3 = 10, then 10 - 5 = 5.
The answer: 13 - 8 = 5.

Exercise II

9 + 2 = 11	11 - 1 = 10	13 - 3 - 1 = 9
9 + 3 = 12	11 - 1 - 1 = 9	13 - 4 = 9
9 + 5 = 14	11 - 2 = 9	13 - 3 - 2 = 8
8 + 3 = 11	3 - 1 - 2 = 0	13 - 5 = 8
8 + 4 = 12	2 + 1 = 3	15 - 5 - 1 = 9
8 + 5 = 13	11 - 1 - 2 = 8	15 - 6 = 9
8 + 7 = 15	12 - 2 - 1 = 9	15 - 5 - 5 = 5
7 + 6 = 13	12 - 3 = 9	15 - 10 = 5

Exercise III

What is 11 minus 1?	*Ans:* 10
What is 11 minus 2?	*Ans:* 9
What is 11 minus 10?	*Ans:* 1
What is 12 minus 1?	*Ans:* 11
What is 12 minus 2?	*Ans:* 10
What is 12 minus 3?	*Ans:* 9
What is 12 minus 4?	*Ans:* 8
What is 12 minus 10?	*Ans:* 2
What is 13 minus 3?	*Ans:* 10
What is 13 minus 4?	*Ans:* 9
What is 13 minus 5?	*Ans:* 8
What is 13 minus 10?	*Ans:* 3
What is 14 minus 4?	*Ans:* 10
What is 14 minus 5?	*Ans:* 9
What is 14 minus 6?	*Ans:* 8
What is 14 minus 10?	*Ans:* 4
What is 15 minus 5?	*Ans:* 10
What is 15 minus 6?	*Ans:* 9

Exercise IV

$12 - 1 = 11$	$14 - 4 = 10$	$12 - 4 = 8$	$14 - 3 - 3 - 3 = 5$
$10 - 2 = 8$	$14 - 5 = 9$	$12 - 8 = 4$	$14 - 4 - 4 = 6$
$10 - 3 = 7$	$14 - 6 = 8$	$14 - 6 = 8$	$14 - 5 - 5 = 4$
$12 - 2 = 10$	$15 - 5 = 10$	$14 - 5 = 9$	$15 - 5 - 5 - 5 = 0$
$13 - 3 = 10$	$15 - 4 = 11$	$13 - 6 = 7$	$15 - 2 - 2 - 2 = 9$
$12 - 3 = 9$	$14 - 2 = 12$	$15 - 9 = 6$	$15 - 3 - 3 - 3 = 6$
$12 - 4 = 8$	$15 - 3 = 12$	$13 - 9 = 4$	$15 - 4 - 4 - 4 = 3$
$12 - 5 = 7$	$15 - 6 = 9$	$12 - 9 = 3$	$15 - 1 - 2 - 3 - 4 = 5$
$11 - 4 = 7$	$15 - 7 = 8$	$12 - 3 - 3 = 6$	$15 - 3 - 4 - 5 = 3$
$13 - 4 = 9$	$15 - 8 = 7$	$12 - 2 - 2 - 2 = 6$	$14 - 5 - 4 - 3 - 2 = 0$
$13 - 2 = 11$	$14 - 7 = 7$	$13 - 2 - 2 - 2 = 7$	$12 - 1 - 2 - 3 - 4 = 2$
$13 - 5 = 8$	$12 - 6 = 6$	$12 - 4 - 4 = 4$	$14 - 7 - 7 = 0$
$13 - 6 = 7$	$12 - 7 = 5$	$12 - 6 - 6 = 0$	$12 - 7 + 4 = 9$
$13 - 7 = 7$	$12 - 5 = 7$	$13 - 3 - 3 - 3 = 4$	$11 - 7 + 3 = 7$

Exercise V

By how much is 12 larger than 8?	*Ans:* 4
By how much is 11 larger than 4?	*Ans:* 7
By how much is 14 larger than 7?	*Ans:* 7
By how much is 15 larger than 8?	*Ans:* 7
By how much is 13 larger than 5?	*Ans:* 8
By how much is 13 larger than 9?	*Ans:* 4
By how much is 11 larger than 8?	*Ans:* 3
By how much is 15 larger than 9?	*Ans:* 6
By how much is 13 larger than 7?	*Ans:* 6

Word Problems

1. Out of 10 pencils in the box, only 5 are sharp. How many are not sharp? *Ans:* 5 pencils are dull.

2. There were 10 pictures in the album. I took out 2. How many pictures are left in the album? *Ans:* 8 pictures.

3. The team has 12 players. 9 players came on time. How many came late? *Ans:* 3 players.

4. It is 11 o'clock. The grandfather clock chimed 8 times. How many chimes are left to chime? *Ans:* 3 times.

5. Out of 12 problems on the test, Cole only finished 7. How many problems didn't he finish? *Ans:* 5 problems.

6. George bought a dozen eggs. On the way home 4 eggs hatched. How many unhatched eggs did he bring home?
Ans: 8 eggs. Remember, one dozen means 12.

7. I will turn 10 years old in 7 months. How old am I?
Ans: I am 9 years old now, because it takes 12 months to make 1 year.

8. My sister is 13 years old. How old was she 3 years ago? *Ans:* 10 years old.
a) How old was she 5 years ago? *Ans:* 8 years old.
b) How old was she 6 years ago? *Ans:* 7 years old.
c) How old was she 10 years ago? *Ans:* 3 years old.

9. My cousin is 14 and I am only 6. How many years older is he than I? *Ans:* 8 years.

10. Jill can drink her orange juice in 13 sips. She already sipped 9 times. How many sips are left to finish her drink? *Ans:* 4 sips.

11. The lunch set has 4 spoons, 4 forks and 4 knifes. How many items does the lunch set have? *Ans:* 12 items.

12. There are 12 items in the set and we used 6. How many are left? *Ans:* 6 items.

13. There are 11 miles between my house and my grandparents' house. My sister dropped me off 9 miles from grandma's house. How many miles do I have to walk to her house? *Ans:* 2 miles.

14. There are 15 rows in the theater; 6 rows are filled. How many rows are empty? *Ans:* 9 rows.

15. Hannah always takes a break after finishing 8 problems. She has 14 problems to do. How many problems will she do after the break? *Ans:* 6 problems.

16. When young Newton sat under the tree, 12 apples fell down. He ate 4 and took home 2. How many did he leave under the tree? *Ans:* 6 apples. He did not think about gravity that day.

17. Fifteen ducklings swam in a pond. 4 went to the shore and 1 walked away to look for his mommy duck. How many ducklings are still in the pond? *Ans:* 10 ducklings.

18. Thirteen dogs came to the park: 3 retrievers, 3 poodles and the rest were mutts. How many mutts came to the park? *Ans:* 7 mutts.

19. In a potato race, Luther missed 4 out of 12 potatoes. How many did he pick up? *Ans:* 8 potatoes.

20. For my birthday, I received $10 from my sister and $5 from my brother. I have already spent $7. How much is left from my birthday present? *Ans:* $8.

21. I am 9 years old. In how many years will I turn 11? *Ans:* 2 years.
    a) In how many years will I turn 13? *Ans:* 4 years.
    b) In how many years will I turn 15? *Ans:* 6 years.
    c) In how many years will I turn 12? *Ans:* 3 years.

22. During the competition, the best stone throw was 13 meters and the worst was 8. What's the difference between the best and worst throw? *Ans:* 5 meters.

23. If I need $6 more to pay for my $12 ticket, how much money do I have now? *Ans:* $6.

24. All 14 plants in my class must be watered. I watered 7, Lisa watered 4, and Sean watered only 3. How many more plants are left to be watered? *Ans:* None, it's all done.

25. There are 6 houses on the left side of the street and 7 on the right. Bella sold Girl Scouts cookies to 5 houses. How many more houses does she have to visit on her street? *Ans:* 8 houses.

26. Morris planted 8 tomatoes on one side of the yard and 5 tomatoes on the other. Only 10 tomatoes grew. How many did not grow? *Ans:* 3 tomatoes.

27. A team has 12 players but only 8 team shirts. How many shirts are missing? *Ans:* 4 shirts.

28. There are 10 letters in a secret code for the secret safe. I only remember 7. How many more letters do I need to remember to open the secret safe? *Ans:* 3 letters.

29. Pablo picked up 11 shirts and put them in the hamper together with 4 other shirts. How many shirts are in the hamper? *Ans:* 15 shirts.

30. There were 15 swans on the lake. 7 swans flew south, 8 went north. How many swans are on the lake now? *Ans:* 0 swans or none.

31. Fred caught 5 bluefish and 7 bass in the lake. He let 2 bluefish and 3 bass go because they were too small. How many fish did he bring home? *Ans:* 7 fish.

32. Noah printed 13 "lost dog" flyers and posted 6. How many more flyers are left to post? *Ans:* 7 flyers. I hope he finds his dog.

33. Twelve runners ran the marathon. First, 3 runners got tired and stopped and then another 3 runners got tired and quit. Then 3 more runners got hurt and stopped. How many runners finished the race? *Ans:* 3 runners.

34. We donated our old clothes. I gave 3 shirts and 4 pairs of pants. Tina gave 5 dresses and 2 sweaters. How many items did we give? *Ans:* 14 items.

35. I took $15 and bought a $5 ticket for Adam and another $5 ticket for Brianna. How much money is left for me to buy a ticket? *Ans:* $5.

36. For the school talent show, I wrote 6 poems and 9 songs. I only sang 4 songs and recited 3 poems. How many poems and songs do I have left for the next show? *Ans:* 8 (6 + 9 - 4 - 3 = 8).

37. I invited some friendly monsters into my room. At first, 5 red monsters came, then 6 green monsters came, then 2 yellow monsters came and 3 green monsters ran away. How many people are in the room?
Ans: Only 1, me. Tricky!!! Monsters are not real; they are not people.

38. There are 13 stripes on the American flag. There are 7 red stripes. How many white stripes are on the flag? *Ans:* 6. By the way, did you know that 13 stripes on the flag represent the 13 original colonies.

39. Calvin roasted 15 chestnuts. He put 8 in one paper bag and the rest in another. How many roasted chestnuts went into the second bag? *Ans:* 7 chestnuts.

40. There are 13 children on my street. 7 kids ride bicycles, and the rest prefer scooters. How many children ride scooters? *Ans:* 6 children.

41. There were 7 children in the figure skating class, then 6 more joined. How many children are in the class? *Ans:* 13 children.

42. The first night, 4 mosquitoes bit Phyllis 6 times. The second night, 5 mosquitoes bit her 7 times. How many times was she bitten? *Ans:* 13 times. Remember, we are counting the bites not mosquitoes.

43. A break lasts 15 minutes. If I take 9 minutes to play ball, how much time will be left? *Ans:* 6 minutes.

44. A year has 12 months. We go to school 9 months. How many months we are on vacation? *Ans:* 3 months.

45. There were 14 children in the karate class. 5 children quit after getting red-belt. How many children stayed to get black-belts? *Ans:* 9 children.

46. A messenger had to deliver 12 packages. She delivered 6 in the morning and 3 in the afternoon. How many more are left to be delivered? *Ans:* 3 packages.

47. A bicyclist rode 14 miles: 5 miles uphill, 6 miles downhill and the rest with on flat ground. How many miles did he ride on flat ground? *Ans:* 3 miles.

48. Rolando had 7 pencils. He bought some more and now he has 11. How many pencils did he buy? *Ans:* 4 pencils.

49. Lynn read 13 books. Mary read 5 less. How many books did Mary read? *Ans:* 8 books.

50. A team needed 15 players. It only found 9. How many more are needed? *Ans:* 6 players.

51. A professor received 14 pieces of mail. There were 5 letters, 4 postcards and the rest were journals. How many journals were there? *Ans:* 5 journals. A journal is a magazine that has articles about a special subject.

52. Paul blew 12 soap bubbles. Paula blew 3 less than Paul. How many bubbles did Paula blow? *Ans:* 9 bubbles.

53. How many doughnuts are 7 doughnuts plus 6 doughnuts? *Ans:* 13 doughnuts.

54. Amy and Ann were jumping rope. Ann jumped 13 times and Amy jumped 7 times. How many times more did Ann jump than Amy? *Ans:* 6 times.

55. Gail joins a game of jackstraws. She draws 7 straws and 5 more later. How many straws does she have? *Ans:* 12 straws.

56. Michael and Nancy put their money together to buy flowers. Michael has $7. Nancy has $6. The flowers cost $15. How much more money do they need? *Ans:* $2.

57. Dina's mom is 5 feet tall. Her dad is 6 feet tall. If Dina's mom stands on her dad's head, how tall will they be? *Ans:* 11 feet.

58. Sevi made 7 glasses of lemonade. Then she made 5 more. She sold 6 glasses of lemonade. How many glasses weren't sold? *Ans:* 6 glasses.

Addition and subtraction up to 15

Exercise I

Count forward from 0 to 14 by adding 2(i.e., 2, 4, 6, 8, etc.)
Count forward from 0 to 15 by adding 3 (i.e., 3, 6, 9, etc.)
Count forward from 0 to 12 by adding 4 (i.e., 4, 8, etc.)
Count forward from 0 to 15 by adding 5 (i.e., 5, 10, 15)
Count backward from 15 to 0 by taking away 3 (15, 12, 9, etc.)
Count backward from 15 to 3 by taking away 4 (15, 11, 7, 3)
Count backward from 15 to 1 by taking away 2 (15, 13, 11, 9, etc.)
Count backward from 15 to 0 by taking away 5 (15, 10, 5, 0)

Exercise II

3 + 3 + 3 = 9	7 + 5 - 4 = 8	7 + 4 - 8 = 3	12 - 5 + 4 = 11
4 + 5 + 3 = 12	4 + 4 + 4 = 12	6 + 7 - 9 = 4	14 - 5 = 9
6 + 7 - 1 = 12	12 - 6 = 6	3 + 6 = 9	15 - 6 = 9
5 + 7 - 3 = 9	9 + 3 - 7 = 5	9 + 5 = 14	4 + 8 - 9 = 3
4 + 9 - 3 = 10	5 + 5 = 10	7 - 3 + 4 = 8	7 + 5 - 10 = 2
12 - 3 = 9	9 + 3 - 6 = 6	11 - 9 + 5 = 7	6 + 5 - 7= 4
10 - 2 = 8	6 + 5 + 4 = 15	12 - 8 + 6 = 10	4 + 5 + 6 = 15

Exercise III

What number and 2 make 10?   *Ans:* 8
What number and 5 make 10?   *Ans:* 5
What number and 7 make 10?   *Ans:* 3
What number and 6 make 10?   *Ans:* 4
What number and 3 make 10?   *Ans:* 7
What number and 2 make 10?   *Ans:* 8
What number and 4 make 10?   *Ans:* 6
What number and 8 make 10?   *Ans:* 2

What number and 3 make 14?	*Ans:* 11
What number and 5 make 14?	*Ans:* 9
What number and 7 make 14?	*Ans:* 7
What number and 8 make 14?	*Ans:* 6
What number and 6 make 12?	*Ans:* 6
What number and 4 make 12?	*Ans:* 8
What number and 5 make 12?	*Ans:* 7
What number and 3 make 12?	*Ans:* 9
What number and 4 make 13?	*Ans:* 9
What number and 6 make 13?	*Ans:* 7
What number and 5 make 13?	*Ans:* 8
What number and 7 make 13?	*Ans:* 6

Exercise IV

What number do you take away from 10 to make 8?	*Ans:* 2
What number do you take away from 11 to make 8?	*Ans:* 3
What number do you take away from 10 to make 6?	*Ans:* 4
What number do you take away from 12 to make 6?	*Ans:* 6
What number do you take away from 11 to make 8?	*Ans:* 3
What number do you take away from 12 to make 3?	*Ans:* 9
What number do you take away from 10 to make 5?	*Ans:* 5
What number do you take away from 11 to make 7?	*Ans:* 4
What number do you take away from 12 to make 5?	*Ans:* 7
What number do you take away from 11 to make 3?	*Ans:* 8
What number do you take away from 10 to make 3?	*Ans:* 7
What number do you take away from 11 to make 5?	*Ans:* 6
What do you get when you take 5 from 11?	*Ans:* 6
What do you get when you take 4 from 11?	*Ans:* 7
What do you get when you take 5 from 9?	*Ans:* 4
What do you get when you take 8 from 12?	*Ans:* 4

Word Problems

1. What is the largest single (one) digit number? *Ans:* 9.

2. Glenn is 12 years old. How old was he 4 years ago? *Ans:* 8 years old.
    a) How old was he 6 years ago? *Ans:* 6 years old.
    b) How old was he 11 years ago? *Ans:* 1 year old.
    c) How old was he 7 years ago? *Ans:* 5 years old.

3. Ann gave $7 to the school fund. Ben gave enough to make the school fund $12 total. How much money did Ben give? *Ans:* $5.

4. There were 9 boats sailing on the lake. Then, 2 boats came back to shore and 3 new boats went out. How many boats are on the lake now? *Ans:* 10 boats (9 - 2 + 3 = 10).

5. Morgan slept 7 hours today. Usually, he sleeps 9 hours. How much less did he sleep today? *Ans:* 2 hours.

6. A zoo had 13 animals from Africa. There were 4 giraffes, 2 zebras and the rest were African elephants. How many African elephants did the zoo have? *Ans:* 7 elephants. Can you tell the difference between an elephant from Africa and one from India?

7. The zoo also had 5 chimps. 7 more were brought in from Africa. How many chimps are in the zoo now? *Ans:* 12 chimps.

8. If there were 7 koi fish in the pond and we added 7 more, how many koi fish are in the pond? *Ans:* 14 koi fish.

9. Dad said to Amy, "There are 6 of us and everyone rides a bicycle. How many wheels do all the bicycles have together?" *Ans:* 12 wheels.
    If the problem is too difficult for a child, count first all the front wheels (six) and then add the back wheels (six).

10. Mother said to Amy, "There are 6 of us in the family. We invited 6 guests for dinner, but 2 couldn't come. How many dinner plates do we need?" *Ans:* 10 dinner plates.
    Solution: 6 members of the family + 6 invited guests = 12 people to be at the dinner. Now, 12 guests invited - 2 guests who couldn't come = 10 people and 10 dinner plates.

11. Amy needed 12 place cards for dinner guests. By the time dinner started, she had only made 4 cards. How many more cards does she need to make? *Ans:* 8 cards.

12. The Little Star twinkled 3 times and then 9 times more. How many times did the Star twinkle? *Ans:* 12 times.

13. Sarah picked 6 berries from one bush and 6 from another bush. Her pet squirrel grabbed 3 berries and ran away. How many berries did she put on the plate? *Ans:* 9 (6 + 6 = 12, then 12 - 3 = 9).

14. If Nina had 5 presents for the family and 7 for her friends, but only wrapped 4, how many more does she need to wrap?
    Ans: 8 more presents to be wrapped (5 + 7 = 12, then 12 - 4 = 8).

15. On Sunday, Bobby spent 3 hours doing his homework, 4 hours playing outside and 2 hours helping mom. How many hours was he busy? *Ans:* 9 hours.

16. Tom's mom gave him 5 new toys and his dad gave him 7 more. How many new toys does he have? *Ans:* 12 toys.

17. A spider frightened little Miss Muffet and liked it so much that he invited 11 spider-friends. How many spiders are there to scare Miss Muffet now? *Ans:* 12 spiders. Would you be scared of 12 spiders?

18. Glenn had $4; he made another $4 more babysitting and then $4 more cleaning the garden. How much money does he have? *Ans:* $12.
    If you were Glenn, what would you do with the money?

19. Cory blew 5 balloons and Dana blew 6. At night 4 balloons popped. How many balloons were left? *Ans:* 7 balloons (5 + 6 = 11, then 11 - 4 = 7).

20. There were 9 tons of hay in a barn; 5 more were brought in but 4 were taken away. How many tons of hay are in the barn? *Ans:* 10 tons of hay.

21. Of the 15 people who were expected for a race, 4 called to say they couldn't come. How many people came to the race? *Ans:* 11 people.

22. If I took 9 apples from the bag and there are 4 apples still inside, then how many were there to begin with? *Ans:* 13 apples.

    Solution: This is a bit difficult problem because it makes you think algebraically. Nonetheless, if there are 9 apples out (I took them out) + 4 apples in (I did not take them), then altogether 9 + 4 = 13 apples inside and outside the bag.

23. Dad cut a piece of garden hose into two pieces. One part is 8 feet long, and the other is 5 feet long. How long was the hose before dad cut it? *Ans:* 13 feet.

24. I picked 5 roses, 5 daisies and 5 peonies. How many flowers did I pick? *Ans:* 15 flowers.

25. In our garden we have 4 oak trees, 4 maple trees and 4 birch trees. How many trees are in the garden? *Ans:* 12 trees.

26. If 14 points were scored in the game by both teams and our team scored 7, how many points did the other team score?
    Ans: 7. Who won? It was a draw.

27. Take the number 4. Add 4 and then add 7. Now take away 10. What number did you get? *Ans:* 5 (4 + 4 = 8,   8 + 7 = 15,   15 - 10 = 5).

28. Out of 14 berries, the chef threw away 3 that were rotten and 2 that were squishy. How many berries were left for the fruit tart? *Ans:* 9 berries.

29. In the zoo, one alligator is 13 feet long and another is only 8 feet. By how many feet is one alligator bigger than the other? *Ans:* By 5 feet.

30. The wind blew 6 oak leaves and 7 maple leaves. A squirrel picked up 9 leaves. How many are still on the ground? *Ans:* 4 leaves.

31. Brett's birthday is on the 12th of the month. Today is the 3rd. How many days left before Brett's birthday? *Ans:* 9 days.

32. There are 9 rocks on one side of the street and 5 rocks on the other. How many rocks are there in total? *Ans:* 14 rocks.

33. How many hours together are 8 hours and 6 hours? *Ans:* 14 hours.

34. A forward kicked the ball 6 times during the first half of the soccer game and 7 times in the second half. He missed the goal 9 times. How many times did he score? *Ans:* 4 times.

35. A tree was cut into three pieces. The first piece was 2 feet, the second piece was 7 feet and the last piece was 5 feet. How long was the whole tree? *Ans:* 14 feet.

36. Elsa and Fred together have $14. Elsa has $8. How much does Fred have? *Ans:* $6.

37. Three blind mice bumped into 11 blind rats. How many blind rodents are there? *Ans:* 14 rodents. What is a rodent?

38. Two rooms have 12 chairs. If the first room has 7 chairs, how many chairs are in the second room? *Ans:* 5 chairs.

39. Luke and Mike bought a soccer ball for $13. Luke paid $11. How much did Mike pay? *Ans:* $2.

40. Old King Cole called for 12 fiddlers but only 3 showed up. How many didn't come? *Ans:* 9 fiddlers. They are in big trouble, I think.

41. A jockey rode a new horse 15 times. He fell off the horse 6 times. How many times did he stay in the saddle? *Ans:* 9 times.

42. There were 6 mangoes in one box and 8 mangoes in the other. Juan put all the mangoes in one box and then took out 5. How many mangoes were left in the box? *Ans:* 9 mangoes (6 + 8 = 14, 14 - 5 = 9).

43. A shoemaker had 14 shoes to repair. After he repaired 8 shoes, 7 more were brought in. How many shoes are there to be fixed now? *Ans:* 13 shoes. *Solution:* 14 shoes to be fixed - 8 shoes he already repaired = 6 shoes. Then 6 shoes + 7 shoes brought in = 13 shoes.

44. A doctor had 14 patients in the waiting room. After she saw 9 patients, 6 new patients walked in. How many patients are in the waiting room now? *Ans:* 11 patients.

45. A cockroach ran a path. He ran 8 feet, then ran back 2 feet. And then he ran 5 feet forward. How many feet forward did he run?
Ans: 11 feet (8 - 2 = 6, 6 + 5 = 11).

46. Dee bought 12 balloons for her birthday. On the way home, 8 balloons flew away. Then she went back and brought home 7 more balloons. How many balloons does she have now? *Ans:* 11 balloons.

47. A sailor tied together two ropes that were 8 feet and 5 feet long. Then, he cut 3 feet from the new rope. How long is the rope now?
Ans: 10 feet (8 + 5 = 13, then 13 - 3 = 10).

48. A trained seal balanced 3 balls on his right flipper, 4 balls on his left flipper and 6 balls on his nose. Then, all the balls except 2 on his nose fell down. How many balls fell?
Ans: 11 balls (3 + 4 + 6 = 13, then 13 - 2 = 11).

49. Shanon and Shawn bought a soccer ball for $23. Shawn paid $11. How much did Shanon pay? *Ans:* $12.

50. The school principal will give a Falcon award if a student does 10 good deeds. June has 3 more good deeds to do before she gets the award. How many good deed has she already done? *Ans:* 7 good deeds.

Addition and subtraction up to 17

Exercise I

10 + 6 = 16	16 - 7 = 9	14 - 9 = 5	14 - 7 - 7 = 0
10 + 6 - 5 = 11	16 - 5 = 11	16 - 7 = 9	14 - 4 - 10 = 0
10 + 7 = 17	7 + 7 = 14	16 - 9 = 7	12 - 6 - 6 = 0
10 + 4 + 3 = 17	8 + 8 = 16	16 - 10 = 6	13 - 6 = 7
10 + 2 + 5 = 17	7 + 8 = 15	16 - 5 = 11	13 - 6 - 5 = 2
10 + 2 + 4 = 16	14 - 7 = 7	16 - 11 = 5	15 - 7 = 8
11 + 1 + 1 = 13	14 - 7 + 2 = 9	12 - 11 = 1	15 - 7 - 8 = 0
11 + 2 + 2 = 15	16 - 7 = 9	13 - 4 = 9	17 - 5 = 12
11 + 2 + 3 = 16	16 - 8 = 8	13 - 9 = 4	17 - 7 = 10
11 + 3 + 3 = 17	15 - 7 = 8	15 - 5 = 10	17 - 8 = 9
14 - 5 = 9	16 - 10 = 6	15 - 6 = 9	17 - 9 = 8
11 + 5 + 1 = 17	16 - 9 = 7	15 - 9 = 6	16 - 9 = 7
15 - 6 = 9	14 - 5 = 9	14 - 9 = 5	16 - 7 - 8 = 1

Problem Solving

Problem: What is 14 - 12 = ?
Solution: Step 1: 12 is equal 10 + 2, then
Step 2: 14 - 12 can be thought of as 14 - 10 - 2
Step 3: 14 - 10 = 4, 4 - 2 = 2
Therefore: 14 - 12 = 2.

Exercise II

11 - 10 = 1	15 - 15 = 0	17 - 5 = 12	14 - 7 = 7
12 - 10 = 2	15 - 8 = 7	17 - 4 = 13	7 + 7 = 14
12 - 11 = 1	16 - 7 = 9	13 - 6 = 7	14 - 8 = 6
13 - 10 = 3	16 - 11 = 5	13 - 7 = 6	14 - 6 = 8
13 - 12 = 1	16 - 2 = 14	6 + 7 = 13	15 - 14 = 1
13 - 11 = 2	13 - 11 = 2	13 - 8 = 5	15 - 11 = 4
14 - 10 = 4	13 - 3 = 10	14 - 5 = 9	15 - 4 = 11
14 - 13 = 1	13 - 10 = 3	14 - 6 = 8	15 - 12 = 3
14 - 12 = 2	13 - 4 = 9	14 - 8 = 6	12 + 3 = 15
14 - 11 = 3	13 - 13 = 0	4 + 9 = 13	15 - 3 = 12
14 - 5 = 9	17 - 7 = 10	8 + 9 = 17	15 - 6 = 9
15 - 10 = 5	17 - 8 = 9	9 + 5 = 14	6 + 9 = 15
15 - 11 = 4	17 - 11 = 6	14 - 5 = 9	16 - 8 = 8
15 - 14 = 1	17 - 12 = 5	14 - 6 = 8	17 - 16 = 1

A trick : Subtracting 9 from a two-digit number:
Problem: What is 15 - 9 = ?
Solution: Step 1: Let's pretend that instead of 9 we subtract 10 from 15.
Then, 15 - 10 = 5. Easy!
Step 2: But we took away 10 which is bigger than 9 by 1.
Now we need to give it back.
5 + 1 = 6.
15 - 9 = 6.

⇨ *The rule: when we take away 9 from a two digit number, it might be easier to take away 10 and then add 1.*

Let's try

13 - 9 = 4	14 - 9 = 5	12 - 9 = 3
17 - 9 = 8	15 - 9 = 6	11 - 9 = 2

Exercise III

12 is made of what number and 5?	*Ans:* 7
15 is made of what number and 4?	*Ans:* 11
14 is made of what number and 5?	*Ans:* 9
15 is made of what number and 10?	*Ans:* 5
16 is made of what number and 11?	*Ans:* 5
13 is made of what number and 5?	*Ans:* 8
14 is made of what number and 6?	*Ans:* 8
11 is made of what number and 5?	*Ans:* 6
12 is made of what number and 9?	*Ans:* 3
14 is made of what number and 7?	*Ans:* 7
16 is made of what number and 9?	*Ans:* 7
15 is made of what number and 7?	*Ans:* 8
10 is made of what number and 5?	*Ans:* 5
13 is made of what number and 6?	*Ans:* 7

Word Problems

1.   There were 6 buttons on my green shirt and 7 on my blue shirt. How many buttons are there on both shirts? *Ans:* 13 buttons.
a) If I lost 5 buttons, how many are still left? *Ans:* 8 buttons.

2.   A concert hall had 7 empty seats in the orchestra and 5 in the balcony. How many empty seats are there? *Ans:* 12 seats.
a) If they sold 9 seats just before the show, how many empty seats are left? *Ans:* 3 seats.

3. There are 9 long nails and 5 short ones in the box. How many nails are in the box altogether? *Ans:* 14 nails.
    a) A carpenter used some and now there are only 6 nails left. How many nails did the carpenter use? *Ans:* 8 nails.

4. One player brought 4 golf balls and another player brought 8 balls for the game. By the end of the game there were only 5 balls left. How many golf balls did the players lose? *Ans:* 7 balls.

5. During the soccer game, our team scored 7 goals and the guest team scored 8. How many goals were scored in the game? *Ans:* 15 goals.
    a) Six goals were scored during the first half of the game. How many goals were scored during the second half? *Ans:* 9 goals.

6. Jamal put 2 ounces of frozen orange juice in a jar and added 12 ounces of water. How many ounces of orange juice did he make? *Ans:* 14 ounces.
    a) Then he drank 8 ounces of the juice. How many ounces are left in a jar? *Ans:* 6 ounces.

7. A photographer took 9 pictures of a smiling baby and 4 pictures of the baby crying. Then she picked 7 good pictures for the family. How many did she throw away? *Ans:* 6 pictures.

8. In the tournament, a tennis player won 5 games and lost 3. There are 15 games altogether in a tournament. How many games are still left to play? *Ans:* 7 games.

9. Gloria baked 7 chocolate chip cookies and Linda baked 6. Together they ate 9. How many cookies did they leave for tomorrow? *Ans:* 4 cookies.

10. I had 5 buttercups, 4 daffodils and 4 roses. I made a bouquet and left out 3 flowers. How many flowers are in my bouquet?
    Ans: 10 flowers (5 + 4 + 4 = 13, then 13 - 3 = 10).

11. There are 7 boys and 8 girls on my team. 6 kids took the bus to go to practice, and the rest of the team walked. How many children walked? *Ans:* 9 children.

12. Yesterday, Victor knew 11 jazz chords and 4 blues chords on his guitar. Today, he forgot 6 chords. How many chords does he remember?
    Ans: 9 cords.

13. A fisherman caught 7 tuna fish and 8 salmon. He threw 4 fish back in the sea. How many did he keep? *Ans:* 11 fish.

14. A week has 7 days. My family went camping for 2 weeks. How many days did we camp? *Ans:* 14 (7 + 7 = 14).

a) We went hiking every day except for the last 3 days. How many days did we hike? *Ans:* 11 (14 - 3 = 11).

15. There were 7 pieces of milk chocolate and 7 pieces of dark chocolate in the box. Now there are only 2 pieces left. How many are missing? *Ans:* 12 pieces. What do you think happened to them?

16. A fisherman caught 8 bluegills and 4 catfish in the lake. He gave 6 fish to his friend. How many did he take home? *Ans:* 6 fish.

17. First, 4 students brought in 6 bags, and 7 janitors brought in 11 bags. Then, 3 teachers took out 9 bags. How many bags are in? *Ans:* 8 bags. Did you get confused? OK, listen to the problem again and pay attention only to the bags and not to the people who carry them (6 + 11 = 17, then 17 - 9 = 8).

18. In a new town, Jordan made 6 new guy friends and 9 new girl friends, but then lost 4 friends. How many friends does Jordan have now? *Ans:* 11 friends.

19. In the backyard, Bobby saw 5 squirrels, 7 gophers and 2 raccoons. How many animals were in the backyard? *Ans:* 14 animals.

20. "Let's measure this triangle," said the teacher. "The first side is 3 inches long, the second is 4 inches long and the third is 5 inches long. What is the length of all 3 sides together? *Ans:* 12 sides. Did you know that the length of all three sides of a triangle is called perimeter? *You may need to show a triangle to help your child with this problem.*

21. Jerry had 7 pencils. He bought some more and now he has 14. How many pencils did he buy? *Ans:* 7 pencils.
    a) Jerry gave away all but 3 pencils. How many did he give away? *Ans:* 11 pencils.

22. Lynn read 13 books. Mary read 5 less than Lynn. How many books did Mary read? *Ans:* 8 books.

23. Sparky, the dog, found 9 bones. Missy, the cat, found 4 less than Sparky. How many bones did they find together? *Ans:* 14 bones.

    Solution: Sparky found 9 bones, Missy found 9 bones - 4 bones = 5 bones. Then, 9 + 5 = 14 bones they found together. What will Missy do with all these bones?

24. Cameron has 8 stamps. Nicole has 5 less. How many stamps do they have together? *Ans:* 11 stamps.

    Solution: Cameron has 8 stamps, Nicole 8 - 5 = 3(stamps). Together they have 8 + 3 = 11(stamps).

25. After boiling 7 eggs, I boiled 7 more. I used 5 boiled eggs for salad. How many boiled eggs do I have now? *Ans:* 9 eggs (7 + 7 = 14, then 14 - 5 = 9).

26. There were 11 children on the playground. After 6 children left, 8 new children came. How many children are on the playground now? *Ans:* 13 kids (11 - 6 = 5, then 5 + 8 = 13).

27. Ruth memorized 6 poems in the morning and 7 poems in the afternoon. The next day, she forgot 12 poems. How many poems did she remember? *Ans:* 1 poem.

28. Andy has 4 carrots, Billy has 5 carrots, and Costa has 14. How many more carrots does Costa have than Andy and Billy put together? *Ans:* 5 carrots.
    Solution: Andy and Billy together have 4 + 5 = 9 carrots.
    Then, 14 (carrots Costa has) - 9(carrots Andy and Billy have together) = 5 carrots. Costa has 5 carrots more than the other two rabbits. I hope you figured out that Andy, Billy, and Costa are rabbits.

29. Eight boys and 7 girls went to the theater. Four children sat in the front row and the rest sat in the second row. How many children sat in the second row? *Ans:* 11 children.

30. Liz bought 4 green balloons, 5 red balloons and 4 pink balloons. On the way home 3 balloons popped. How many made it home safely? *Ans:* 10 balloons (4 + 5 + 4 = 13; then 13 - 3 = 10).

31. I ran 3 flights of stairs. The first flight had 6 steps, the second had only 5, and the third had 4 steps. How many steps were there altogether? *Ans:* 15 steps.

32. Miriam drew 4 pictures and then 9 more. Later, she gave away 6 pictures. How many pictures did she keep? *Ans:* 7 pictures.

33. There were 4 chairs in the living room. We brought in 4 more chairs from one room and 6 chairs from another room. How many chairs are in the living room now? *Ans:* 14 chairs.

34. A truck with a trailer is 16 feet long. The trailer by itself is 5 feet long. How long is the truck? *Ans:* 11 feet.

35. If you take 10 out of 16, how much is left? *Ans:* 6.

36. Two sailors raised 17 flags. The first sailor raised 8 flags. How many did the other sailor raise? *Ans:* 9 flags.

37. Rub-a-dub-dub. There are 3 men in the tub and 13 men outside the tub. How many men are there altogether? *Ans:* 16 men.

38. Zack has 4 shelves with 12 books. Zoë has 12 shelves with 4 books.
   a) How many shelves do they both have? *Ans:* 16 shelves.
   b) How many books do both have? *Ans:* Also 16.

39. Kirk put 5 roses, 4 daisies 3 violets in the vase. The next day, he took 12 flowers out of the vase. How many flowers did he leave in the vase? *Ans:* None.

40. Clair's Halloween costume had 2 huge buttons, 7 big buttons, 3 small buttons, and 1 tiny button. After trick-or-treating, she noticed that 5 buttons were missing. How many buttons are now on the costume? *Ans:* 8 buttons.

   Solution: Let's count: 2 + 7 is 9; plus 3 makes it 12, plus 1 makes it 13. There were 13 buttons on the costume. Clair lost 5. 13 - 5 = 8.

41. Grandma baked 7 apple pies and 8 cookies. We ate all the apple pies and only 3 cookies. How many apple pies and cookies are left? *Ans:* 5 cookies. There are no apple pies since we ate them all.

42. There were 7 nails and 6 screws in the box. Anna took out 4 nails and 4 screws. How many nails and screws are left? *Ans:* 5.

   Solutions: There are 2 ways to solve this problem
   One Way: There were 7 nails and Anna took out 4, then 7 - 4 = 3; there are 3 nails left in the box. There were 6 screws and Anna took out 6, 6 - 4 = 2, there are 2 screws left. Now, there are together 3 nails and 2 screws, 3 + 2 = 5
   Another Way: There were 7 nails and 6 screws together. 7 + 6 = 13. Anna took out 4 nails. 13 - 4 = 9; She also took 4 screws. 9 - 4 = 5. The answer is 5 either way.

43. Joyce made 4 turkey sandwiches and 7 cheese sandwiches. The family ate all the turkey sandwiches and 2 cheese sandwiches. How many sandwiches are left? *Ans:* 5 sandwiches.

   Solution: There were 4 + 7 = 11 (sandwiches), 11 - 4 - 2 = 5 (sandwiches).

44. Sandy had $8 in her left pocket and $4 in her right pocket. After she paid for cat food with $5 from the left pocket and $3 from the right, how much money does she have? *Ans:* $4.

   Solution: One way to do it: 8 + 4 = 12, then 12 - 5 - 3 = 4.
   The other way: In the left pocket: 8 - 5 = 3; In the right pocket: 4 - 3 = 1
   In both pockets now after Sandy paid for the cat food: 3 + 1 = 4

45. Henry won 6 awards. Ali won 3 more than Henry. How many awards did they win together? *Ans:* 15 awards.

   Solution: Ali has 6 + 3 = 9 awards. Both boys have 6 + 9 = 15 awards.

46. The earrings and the necklace cost $16. The necklace is $11. How much were the earrings? *Ans:* $5.

47. Trish picked 4 apples, 5 pears and 6 lemons. Out of these she took 14 fruits to the neighbor. How many fruits did she keep for herself?
Ans: 1 fruit.

A challenge

49. There are 8 miles from the actor's house to the movie set. The actor drove 3 miles and then remembered that he left the movie script at home. He went back home and then drove all the way to the set. How many miles did the actor drive? *Ans:* 14 miles.

Solution: First the actor drove 3 miles; then he drove back 3 miles, that makes 6. Then he had to start all over again and drove 8 miles to the set. 6 + 8 = 14 miles.

Addition up to 20
and adding equal numbers

Exercise I

10 + 1 = 11	12 + 2 = 14	12 + 2 = 14	14 + 2 = 16
10 + 2 = 12	12 + 6 = 18	12 + 4 = 16	14 + 3 = 17
10 + 3 = 13	12 + 8 = 20	12 + 5 = 17	14 + 4 = 18
10 + 5 = 15	13 + 1 = 14	12 + 6 = 18	14 + 2 = 16
11 + 3 = 14	13 + 3 = 16	12 + 7 = 19	14 + 5 = 19
11 + 4 = 15	13 + 6 = 19	13 + 3 = 16	14 + 6 = 20
11 + 6 = 17	15 + 2 = 17	13 + 4 = 17	15 + 2 = 17
11 + 8 = 19	15 + 4 = 9	13 + 5 = 18	15 + 3 = 18
11 + 9 = 20	15 + 5 = 20	13 + 6 = 19	15 + 4 = 19
12 + 1 = 13	19 + 1 = 20	13 + 7 = 20	15 + 5 = 20

Exercise II

What do you add to 19 to make 20?	*Ans:* 1
What do you add to 18 to make 20?	*Ans:* 2
What do you add to 10 to make 20?	*Ans:* 10
What do you add to 15 to make 20?	*Ans:* 5
What do you add to 16 to make 20?	*Ans:* 4
What do you add to 12 to make 20?	*Ans:* 8
What do you add to 11 to make 20?	*Ans:* 9
What do you add to 9 to make 20?	*Ans:* 11
What do you add to 8 to make 20?	*Ans:* 12
What do you add to 14 to make 20?	*Ans:* 6
What do you add to 1 to make 20?	*Ans:* 19
What do you add to 3 to make 20?	*Ans:* 17
What do you add to 17 to make 20?	*Ans:* 3
What do you add to 13 to make 20?	*Ans:* 7
What do you add to 6 to make 16?	*Ans:* 10
What do you add to 0 to make 20?	*Ans:* 20
What do you add to 17 to make 19?	*Ans:* 2
What do you add to 13 to make 16?	*Ans:* 3
What do you add to 16 to make 19?	*Ans:* 3
What do you add to 12 to make 19?	*Ans:* 7
What do you add to 14 to make 19?	*Ans:* 5

Exercise III

10 + 6 = 16	13 + 6 = 19	6 + 3 + 9 = 18	15 + 5 = 20
10 + 9 = 19	2 + 14 = 16	6 + 3 + 7 = 16	14 + 6 = 20
10 + 10 = 20	6 + 14 = 20	4 + 5 + 6 = 15	17 + 2 = 19
4 + 10 = 14	15 + 2 = 17	5 + 6 + 7 = 18	11 + 9 = 20
7 + 10 = 17	5 + 15 = 20	6 + 6 + 6 = 18	13 + 5 = 18
0 + 19 = 19	15 + 3 = 18	7 + 6 + 5 = 18	12 + 6 = 18
11 + 2 = 13	19 + 1 = 20	5 + 5 + 5 = 15	9 + 8 = 17
11 + 5 = 16	9 + 6 = 15	3 + 6 + 8 = 17	8 + 9 = 17
11 + 9 = 20	9 + 8 = 17	15 + 1 = 16	8 + 8 = 16
11 + 7 = 18	9 + 9 = 18	15 + 2 = 17	7 + 9 = 16
12 + 4 = 16	2 + 17 = 19	15 + 3 = 18	9 + 9 = 18
12 + 7 = 19	7 + 9 = 16	14 + 2 = 16	10 + 10 = 20
5 + 12 = 17	7 + 8 = 15	14 + 4 = 18	2 + 17 = 19
8 + 12 = 20	4 + 16 = 20	16 + 2 = 18	7 + 8 = 15
13 + 4 = 17	4 + 13 = 17	3 + 16 = 19	6 + 9 = 15
5 + 13 = 18	12 + 7 = 19	15 + 4 = 19	5 + 6 + 1 = 12
7 + 13 = 20	7 + 8 + 2 = 17	17 + 3 = 20	7 + 3 + 3 = 13

Exercise IV

6 + 6 = 12	9 + 9 = 18	6 + 6 + 6 = 18
7 + 7 = 14	10 + 10 = 20	4 + 4 + 4 + 4 = 16
8 + 8 = 16	5 + 5 + 5 = 15	5 + 5 + 5 + 5 = 20

Learn a Trick

When adding 3 or more numbers, sometimes it makes it easier to rearrange them. For example: let's say we need to solve 9 + 7 + 1. Of course, 9 + 7 = 16, then 16 + 1 = 17. Correct.
A simpler way might be to do first 9 + 1 = 10, and then 10 + 7 = 17.

Now you try it.
5 + 8 + 2 = ?   Think (8 + 2) + 5 = 15

5 + 8 + 5 = ?	Think (5 + 5) + 8 = 18		
2 + 9 + 8 = ?	*Ans:* 19	4 + 9 + 6 = ?	*Ans:* 19
9 + 9 + 1 = ?	*Ans:* 19	8 + 9 + 2 = ?	*Ans:* 19
3 + 5 + 4 + 5 = ?	*Ans:* 17	7 + 7 + 3 = ?	*Ans:* 17

Word Problems

1. Sarah invited 14 friends to her party, but 5 more than she invited showed up. How many friends came to the party? *Ans:* 19 friends.

2. A broken clock struck 12 times and then 5 more times. How many times did the clock strike? *Ans:* 17 times.

3. Chloe did 5 math problems, then 5 more, and then another 5 problems. How many math problems did she do in all? *Ans:* 15 problems.

4. It rained for 14 days and then for another 6 more days after that. How many days did it rain altogether? *Ans:* 20 days.

5. There are 9 books on one shelf and 8 books on the other. How many books are there on both shelves? *Ans:* 17 books.

6. A cat caught 15 mice yesterday and 5 mice today. How many mice did it catch? *Ans:* 20 mice.

7. The mechanic fixed 8 cars today and 8 cars yesterday. How many cars did he fix in the past 2 days? *Ans:* 16 cars.

8. Louis made two bouquets: 12 roses in one and 6 roses in the other. How many roses did he use? *Ans:* 18 roses.

9. The dentist drilled 13 teeth before lunch and 5 more after lunch. How many teeth did he drill? *Ans:* 18 teeth. Ouch!

10. Ernest is 14 years old. How old will he be in 3 years? *Ans:* 17 years.
    a) In 4 years? *Ans:* 18 years.
    b) In 5 years? *Ans:* 19 years.
    c) In 6 years? *Ans:* 20 years.

11. Randy recorded 8 songs for his dad, 6 songs for his mom and 4 songs for himself. How many songs did he record? *Ans:* 18 songs.

12. After a snowstorm, Mr. Miller cleaned his driveway and 18 driveways for his neighbors. How many driveways did he clean altogether?
    Ans: 19 driveways.

13. Ali washed 4 shirts, 5 shorts, and 9 socks. How many pieces of clothing did he wash? *Ans:* 18 pieces of clothing.

14. Today is March 15th. Pauline's birthday is in 4 days. When is her birthday? *Ans:* March 19th.

15. Today is June 13th. The concert is in one week. When is the concert? *Ans:* June 20th.

16. Last week had 7 days and this week also has 7 days. How many days are in both weeks? *Ans:* 14. Any 2 weeks will always have 14 days.

17. I have $4. I need $12 more to buy a book. What's the price of the book? *Ans:* $16.

18. Jill has 9 dolls and Katie has 8. How many dolls do they have together? *Ans:* 17 dolls.

19. On the test, Nancy spelled correctly 8 words and missed 8. How many words were on the test? *Ans:* 16 words.

20. A baseball hat costs $6 and a backpack costs $13. How much do both cost? *Ans:* $19.

21. Cleaning the park, Keith picked up 8 empty cans and Kate picked up 12 cans. How many cans did they pick up together? *Ans:* 20 cans.

22. One room has 10 windows, and the other room also has 10. How many windows are there in both rooms? *Ans:* 20 windows.

23. Everyone in my class has a talent. We have 4 dancers, 8 singers, 3 poets and 4 guitar players. How many kids are in my class? *Ans:* 19 kids.

24. Our team played 15 games. We need 5 more to finish the tournament. How many games altogether do we play? *Ans:* 20 games.

25. There were 9 eggs in one nest and 9 eggs in the other. How many eggs are in both nests? *Ans:* 18 eggs.

26. I ran for 11 minutes, then rested for 5 minutes and then ran again for 2 minutes. How much time did I spend running and resting? *Ans:* 18 minutes (11 + 5 + 2 = 18).

27. There are 8 chairs on one side of the room and 8 chairs on the other. How many chairs are in the room? *Ans:* 16 chairs.

28. There are 5 letters in my first name, 5 letters in my middle name and 5 letters in my last name. How many letters are there in my full name? *Ans:* 15 letters.

29. The girls collected snails in the garden. Kim found 9 snails, Liz found 8 snails, and Mary found none. How many snails did they pick up together? *Ans:* 17 snails.

30. The game was a tie. Each team scored 7 points. How many points were scored by both teams? *Ans:* 14 points.

31. A traveler spent 9 days in one city and 9 days in the other. How many days did she travel? *Ans:* 18 days.

32. A stock costs $14 and went up in price by $4. What is the price of the stock now?
    Ans: $18. As you see, you don't even need to know what a stock is to give the right answer.

33. My dog has 4 legs, my cat has 4 legs, my rabbit has 4 legs, and my hamster has 4 legs. How many legs do all my pets have altogether? *Ans:* 16 legs.

34. Each of my hands has 4 fingers and 1 thumb. My feet have 10 toes altogether. How many fingers, thumbs and toes do I have?
    Ans: 20 fingers, thumbs, and toes together.

35. A dozen means 12. The baker sold a dozen bagels and then 6 more. How many bagels did the baker sell? *Ans:* 18 bagels.

36. There are 6 white, 6 yellow and 6 brown butterflies in the garden. How many butterflies are there? *Ans:* 18 butterflies.

37. Greg carries 9 pounds of apples in one hand and 9 pounds of oranges in the other. How much weight does he carry in both hands?
    Ans: 18 pounds. In this problem we are not adding apples and oranges, only their weight in pounds.

38. A magician pulled 8 rabbits from the left pocket and 8 from the right. How many rabbits did he pull out of his pockets? *Ans:* 16 rabbits.

39. We went to the movies. We bought 2 adult tickets and one child ticket. The adult ticket was $8 and the child ticket was only $4. How much money did we spend on tickets? *Ans:* $20.

    Solution: Two adult tickets were $8 + $8 = $16, $16 + $4 (for child's ticket) = $20.

40. Mother told Dennis 15 times not to tease the dog and then told him 3 more times. How many times did mom ask Dennis to stop teasing the dog? *Ans:* 18 times. Now Dennis is in big trouble.

41. At the beginning of the chess game Peter had 16 pieces. He lost 8. How many pieces does he have now? *Ans:* 8 pieces.

42. If Horace had 12 goldfish and bought 7 more, how many fish does he have? *Ans:* 19 fish.

43. A jeweler added 8 diamonds to a necklace and then 9 more to make it really sparkle. How many diamonds are in the necklace? *Ans:* 17 diamonds.

44. Alex washed 6 plates, 6 saucers and 6 cups. How many pieces of china did he wash? *Ans:* 18 pieces.

45. Yesterday, Ms. Martinez spent $11 dollars on lunch, and today she spent $6. How much did she spend for both lunches? *Ans:* $17.

46. After Ruth became an artist, she made 5 paintings in the first year, 6 in second year and 7 in the third year. How many paintings did Ruth make? *Ans:* 18 paintings (5 + 6 = 11, 11 + 7 = 18).

47. At first, there were 4 kids on the swim team. Then, 5 more joined. After that, 8 new kids joined the team. How big is the team? *Ans:* 17 children.

48. Edith and Amy are jumping rope. Edith jumps 9 times and Amy jumps 6 times. How many times did they both jump? *Ans:* 15 times.

49. Aunt Silvia cut a rope to make two jumping ropes. One piece of rope is 8 feet long, and the other piece is 6 feet. How long was the rope, before Aunt Silvia cut it? *Ans:* 14 feet long.

50. Peter and Will decided to put their money together to buy a football. Peter had $14 and Will had $6. How much do they both have? *Ans:* $20.

51. The boys are getting ready for a snowball fight. One group of 6 boys made 9 balls and the group of 9 boys made 8 balls. How many snowballs did they make in all? *Ans:* 17 snowballs. Remember to count snowballs, not the boys who made them.

52. The coach bought 9 team shirts and 9 matching shorts. How many shirts and shorts did she buy? *Ans:* 18 shirts and shorts.

53. The children are playing store. Little Richard has 7 pine cones, 6 acorns and 5 sticks in his store. How many items are in his store? *Ans:* 18 items.

54. It took two pieces of carpet to cover the room. The first piece was 12 feet long and the other piece was 8 feet long. How many feet of carpet were used? *Ans:* 20 feet.

55. An assistant filed 11 charts under the letter A and 7 charts under the letter B. How many charts did she file? *Ans:* 18 files.

56. When the police caught the thief, he had 11 stolen wallets on him. At his home, they found 8 more. How many wallets did he steal? *Ans:* 19 wallets.

Subtraction with numbers up to 20

Problem Solving

First Problem: What is 18 - 9 = ?

Solution: Step 1: 9 equals to 8 + 1
                    Step 2: We can say then that 18 - 9 is the same as 18 - 8 and then - 1.
                    Step 3: 18 - 8 = 10, 10 - 1 = 9
                    The answer: 18 - 9 = 9.

Second Problem: What is 20 - 7 = ?

Solution: Step 1: 20 equals to 10 + 10
                    Step 2: We can take 7 from the second 10 (or we can do it from the first) and 10 - 7 = 3
                    Step 3: Since we never did anything to the other 10, we can add it back to 3. 3 + 10 = 13
                    The answer: 20 - 7 = 13.

Third Problem: 17 - 13 = ?

Solution: Step 1: 13 equals to 10 + 3
                    Step 2: We can then do first 17 - 10 = 7, and then 7 - 3 = 4
                    The answer: 17 - 13 = 4.

Learning a trick

Subtracting 9 from a number

16 - 9 = ?

Solution: Step 1: Let's pretend that instead of 9 we subtract 10 from 16. Then, 16 - 10 = 6. Easy!
                    Step 2: But we took away 10 which is bigger than 9 by 1. Now we need to give it back.
                    6 + 1 = 7.
                    16 - 9 = 7.

⇨ *The rule:* When we take 9 away from a number, it might be easier to take away 10 first and then add 1.

Exercise I

12 - 11 = 1	16 - 14 = 2	18 - 15 = 3
13 - 12 = 1	16 - 13 = 3	18 - 12 = 6
14 - 11 = 3	17 - 11 = 6	19 - 11 = 8
15 - 10 = 5	17 - 16 = 1	19 - 15 = 4
15 - 11 = 4	17 - 15 = 2	19 - 12 = 7
15 - 12 = 3	17 - 14 = 3	19 - 16 = 3
15 - 13 = 2	17 - 12 = 5	19 - 14 = 5
16 - 11 = 5	18 - 11 = 7	19 - 18 = 1
16 - 15 = 1	18 - 16 = 2	19 - 17 = 2

Exercise II

Count backward from 20 to 0 by 1 (i.e., 20, 19, 18.)
Count backward from 20 to 0 by 2 (i.e., 20, 18, 16.)
Count backward from 20 by 3 (i.e., 20, 17, 14, 11, 8, 5, and 2)
Count backward from 20 by 4 (i.e., 20, 16, 12, 8, 4, and 0)
Count backward from 20 by 5 (i.e., 20, 15, 10, 5, and 0)
Count backward from 20 by 6 (i.e., 20, 14, 8, and 2)
Count backward from 20 by 7 (i.e., 20, 13, and 6)
Count backward from 20 by 8 (i.e., 20, 12, and 4)

Exercise III

20 - 5 = 15	18 - 3 = 15	17 - 12 = 5	15 - 4 = 11
20 - 2 = 18	18 - 5 = 13	17 - 15 = 2	15 - 5 = 10
20 - 1 = 19	18 - 10 = 8	17 - 13 = 4	15 - 6 = 9
20 - 9 = 11	18 - 8 = 10	17 - 16 = 1	15 - 8 = 7
20 - 10 = 10	18 - 2 = 16	17 - 8 = 9	15 - 7 = 8
20 - 7 = 13	18 - 5 = 13	16 - 5 = 11	14 - 8 = 6
19 - 1 = 18	18 - 11 = 7	16 - 11 = 5	13 - 5 = 8
19 - 3 = 16	18 - 7 = 11	12 - 5 = 7	12 - 8 = 4
19 - 5 = 14	18 - 12 = 6	16 - 8 = 8	15 - 6 = 9
19 - 6 = 13	18 - 13 = 5	16 - 12 = 4	11 - 3 = 8
19 - 7 = 12	18 - 15 = 3	16 - 13 = 3	13 - 8 = 5
19 - 10 = 9	18 - 17 = 1	16 - 15 = 1	12 - 5 = 7
19 - 11 = 8	17 - 2 = 15	16 - 14 = 2	15 - 8 = 7
19 - 12 = 7	17 - 3 = 14	16 - 9 = 7	14 - 8 = 6
19 - 13 = 6	17 - 6 = 11	17 - 7 = 10	13 - 8 = 5
19 - 14 = 5	17 - 8 = 9	15 - 5 = 10	12 - 8 = 4

Word Problems

1. Tim and I together have 20 concert tickets. I have 10. How many does Tim have? *Ans:* 10 tickets.

2. Two trucks together can carry 20 boxes. One truck can take 12 boxes. How much can the other truck carry? *Ans:* 8 boxes.

3. The sum of two numbers is 20. One number is 11. What's the other number? *Ans:* 9.

4. The sum of two numbers is 20. One number is 7. What's the other number? *Ans:* 13.

5. The sum of two numbers is 20. One number is 5. What's the other number? *Ans:* 15.

6. The sum of two numbers is 20. One number is 4. What's the other number? *Ans:* 16.

7. The sum of two numbers is 20. One number is 3. What's the other number? *Ans:* 17.

8. The sum of two numbers is 20. One number is 16. What's the other number? *Ans:* 4.

9. The sum of two numbers is 20. One number is 18. What's the other number? *Ans:* 2.

10. There are 14 days in 2 weeks. Of these 14 days, children go to school for 10 days. How many days are there when the children don't have to go to school? *Ans:* 4 days.

11. Harry can walk to the store in 17 minutes, but when his mom wants him to hurry, he runs to the store in 5 minutes. How many minutes does he save by running? *Ans:* 12 minutes.

12. Sarah had $19 in her bank. She took out $8 for her father's birthday present. How much money did she leave in the bank? *Ans:* $11.

13. Vic is 19. His sister is only 9. By how many years is Vic older than his sister? *Ans:* 10 years.

14. There are 19 students in my class. The flu kept 10 students at home. How many students came to school? *Ans:* 9 students.

15. There were 17 birds of feather that flocked together. Then, there were only 6. How many decided not to flock? *Ans:* 11 birds.

16. Juanita bought 17 invitations and sent out 8 right away. How many cards are left to be sent? *Ans:* 9 cards.

17. I saved $17 and then spent $11 on a book. How much money is left? *Ans:* $6.

18. Frank keeps an 18-foot long sidewalk clean. After he has swept 12 feet of it, how many feet remain to be swept? *Ans:* 6 feet.

19. For the party, Kevin bakes 17 small pizzas. After the party, there were 5 pizzas left. How many pizzas were eaten? *Ans:* 12 pizzas.

20. There were 19 eggs in the refrigerator. The chef took 12 eggs to make a giant cake. How many eggs were left? *Ans:* 7 eggs.

21. A Lego toy has 20 parts. 15 parts are red and the rest are yellow. How many yellow parts are in the toy? *Ans:* 5 parts.

22. Tracy and I had to feed 18 rabbits. Tracy fed 9 and I fed the rest. How many rabbits did I feed? *Ans:* 9 rabbits.

23. Nora went to buy veggies. She took $20 and brought back $6 change. How much did the veggies cost? *Ans:* $14.

24. Little Bo Peep lost 19 sheep. Then 12 sheep came home wagging their tails behind them. How many didn't come home? *Ans:* 7 sheep. Don't worry, they came home later.

25. Uncle Sid has 18 rose bushes. He pruned 11. How many more does he have to prune? *Ans:* 7 bushes.

26. Lunch break is 19 minutes long. We played dodge-ball for 13 minutes. How many minutes are left to eat lunch? *Ans:* 6 minutes.

27. Uncle Sid asked me to move 16 flower pots to the sunny side of the garden. I moved 8. How many more do I have to move? *Ans:* 8 pots.

28. There are 18 holes on the golf course. After the 9th hole, how many more are left to play? *Ans:* 9 holes.

29. Harrison's kite flew up 17 feet and then went down 6 feet. How high is his kite now? *Ans:* 11 feet.

30. Take all 18 pictures from the wall, my teacher said. I took 9. How many more are still hanging on the wall? *Ans:* 9 pictures.

31. There are 20 children in Angie's class. 12 are boys. How many girls are in her class? *Ans:* 8 girls.
    a) Yesterday, 14 children came to the class. How many did not come? *Ans:* 6 children.

b) Today 13 children came in late. How many came on time?
Ans: 7 children.

32. Out of 19 days in May, it was raining for 10. How many days were dry?
Ans: 9 days.

33. Rhea has 19 rocks for her rock garden. She put 7 rocks on the right and 2 in the middle. How many rocks are on the left side of her garden?
Ans: 10 rocks.

Solution: 19 rocks - 7 rocks (on the right) = 12,
12 rocks - 2 rocks (in the middle) = 10 rocks (left on the left).
There is another way to solve this problem:
First we can add the rocks on the right and in the middle together, because they are not on the left. 7 rocks on the right + 2 rocks in the middle = 9 rocks. Then we can take away 9 rocks from total number of rocks. 19 rocks - 9 rocks that are not on the left = 10 rocks.

34. There are 16 gold fish in Yoshiko's pond. She took 8 gold fish out for second pond. How many fish are left in the first pond? *Ans:* 8 gold fish.

35. From 20 yards of carpet, Keiko cut 9. How many yards are left? *Ans:* 11 yards.

36. Out of 20 ostrich eggs, 7 hatched. How many didn't? *Ans:* 13 eggs.

37. Out of 20 bees in a beehive, 6 are out scouting for flowers. How many stayed in the hive? *Ans:* 14 bees.

38. The fish is 20 inches long. The tail is 4 inches and the head is 5 inches. How long is the fish's body? *Ans:* 11 inches.

Solution: 20 inches (the whole fish, head + body + tail) - 4 inches (tail) = 16 inches. Then, 16 inches - 5 inches (head) = 11 inches (fish's body)

39. It takes Walter 17 minutes to clean his room. He takes 6 minutes to pick up his clothes, 4 minutes to put his books on the shelf, and the rest he spends making his bed. How long does it take Walter to make the bed?
Ans: 7 minutes.

40. There are 18 pages in the story. I read 11 pages yesterday and 3 pages today. How many pages did I leave for tomorrow? *Ans:* 4 pages.

41. Tom put 20 items in the dishwasher. There were 8 forks and 8 spoons, the rest were knives. How many knives did he put in? *Ans:* 4 knives.

Solution: There are 8 forks and 8 spoons; together there are 8 + 8 = 16 utensils that are not knives. There are 20 utensils, 16 are not knives. Then, 20 utensils - 16 not knives = 4 knives.

42. There were 18 peaches on the peach tree. First, 5 peaches fell down, and then 5 more fell down. How many are still on the tree?
Ans: 8 peaches.

43. The store sold 7 pencils and then 7 more pencils. How many more pencils do they need to sell to make it 14?
Ans: 0, because they have already sold all 14 pencils.

44. A basket had 12 tomatoes and 5 cucumbers. Fiona picks 7 vegetables. How many did she leave in the basket? *Ans:* 10 vegetables.

    Solution: 12 vegetables (tomatoes) + 5 vegetables (cucumbers) = 17 vegetables in the basket. Then, 17 vegetables - 7 vegetables = 10 vegetables left.

45. Seventeen tickets were left to be sold. Yolanda sold 13 and then 4 more. How many tickets are still available? *Ans:* 0, she sold them all.

46. Pam put 9 glasses of lemonade in one pitcher and 7 in another. She has sold 4 glasses from each pitcher. How many glasses are left?
Ans: 8 glasses.

    Solution: From the first pitcher: 9 - 4 = 5 glasses are left; from the second 7 - 4 = 3 glasses left. Then, 5 glasses (left in the first pitcher) + 3 glasses (in the second) = 8 glasses (left in both pitchers).

47. There were 8 sheets of white paper and 8 sheets of yellow paper. The store sold 6 sheets of each color. How many sheets of paper are left?
Ans: 4 sheets. (2 white and 2 yellow).

48. Tom had 8 large boxes and 12 small boxes. He used 10 boxes. How many boxes are left? *Ans:* 10 boxes.

49. An airline company has 18 planes; 5 are passenger planes and the rest are cargo. How many cargo planes do they have? *Ans:* 13 planes.

50. A company had an order for 20 tractors. They delivered 17. How many more are left to deliver? *Ans:* 3 tractors.

51. King's mount castle has 20 rooms. The king and the queen vacuumed 14. How many rooms are left to be vacuumed? *Ans:* 6 rooms.

52. Out of 20 jokes the jester told him, the king didn't care for 13. How many jokes did the king like? *Ans:* 7 jokes.

53. There are 20 cats in the king's castle. If 14 cats catch mice, how many don't? *Ans:* 6 cats.

54. There are 20 guards in the castle. If 12 guards are on duty, how many have the day off? *Ans:* 8 guards.

55. An archer shot 20 arrows and hit the target 18 times. How many times did she miss? *Ans:* 2 times.

56. A train has 20 compartments with 7 of them for luggage. How many are for passengers? *Ans:* 13 compartments.

57. Michael had 8 large boxes and 8 small boxes. He used 4 boxes. How many boxes are left? *Ans:* 12 boxes.

58. An tractor company has 18 tractors; 5 are green and the rest are yellow. How many yellow tractors do they have? *Ans:* 13 tractors.

59. A company had an order for 13 tractors. They delivered 7. How many more are left to deliver? *Ans:* 6 tractors.

60. The motel has 20 rooms of which the maid cleaned 14. How many rooms are left to be cleaned? *Ans:* 6 rooms.

The meaning of double and half

Note for the parents: Half might be a difficult concept for young children. If that is the case, skip Exercise I, the explanation and problems 11 to 22.

Double
To double a number means to add the number to itself. If I ask you to double 2, that means 2 + 2, or 4. If you double 3, it means 3 + 3 or 6. If you double 5 it would be 10, because 5 + 5 equals 10.

$$4 + 4 = 8 \qquad 6 + 6 = 12 \qquad 5 + 5 = 10$$
$$7 + 7 = 14 \qquad 8 + 8 = 16 \qquad 9 + 9 = 18$$

What happens if you double 1? *Ans:* 2
What happens if you double 2? *Ans:* 4
What happens if you double 0? *Ans:* 0 because if you add nothing to nothing, it will be nothing

Half
We get half when we break a number in two equal parts. Number 2 is made of 2 equal parts, 1 and 1. That means 1 is one half of 2.

Number 4 is made of 2 equal numbers, 2 and 2. That means that one half of 4 is 2.

Number 10 is made of 2 equal numbers, 5 and 5. That means one half of 10 is 5.

Exercise I

What is one half of 6?   *Ans:* 3.
What is one half of 8?   *Ans:* 4.
What is one half of 12?   *Ans:* 6.
What is one half of 6?   *Ans:* 3.
What is one half of 20?   *Ans:* 10.
What is one half of 0?   *Ans:* 0 because one half of nothing is still nothing.

Note: not all the numbers can have halves. The numbers that do are called even numbers. These numbers are 2, 4, 6, 8, 10, 12, and many others. If a number does not break evenly into two halves, we call it a odd number.

When we try to find one half of an odd number we end up with one part bigger than the other. Try to find one half of 3. It would not work, because the 2 numbers that make 3 - 2 and 1 - are not equal. Later on, we will learn how to find one half of odd (uneven) numbers but for now let's use only even numbers to get halves.

Word Problems

1. Tina has 6 pencils. I gave her some more pencils. Now she has double what she had before. How many pencils did I give her? *Ans:* 6 pencils.

2. Ernie can do 4 push ups. "I can do double that many," said Bart. How many can he do? *Ans:* 8 push ups. How many push ups can you do?

3. I have 5 toes on one foot. On both feet, I have double. How many toes do I have? *Ans:* 10 toes.

4. Nick runs a mile in 6 minutes. For Jim, it takes double this time. How long does it take for Jim to run a mile? *Ans:* 12 minutes.

5. Fran carries 7 pounds. Nan can carry double that much. How much can Nan carry? *Ans:* 14 pounds.

6. Vera fed 4 puppies. Mira fed double that number. How many puppies did Mira feed? *Ans:* 8 puppies.

7. I am 8 years old. I will double my age in 8 years. How old will I be then? *Ans:* 16 years old.

8. Hannah had $10 and doubled her money doing babysitting. How much does she have now? *Ans:* $20.

9. Vince had 6 whammies. Then he doubled them. How many whammies does he have? *Ans:* 12 whammies.

10. What is half of 10? *Ans:* 5.

11. It takes Dolores 8 hours to clean the school yard. If Scott helps her, they can finish in half the time. How long would it take both of them to do the cleaning? *Ans:* 4 hours.

12. I saw my cousin holding 8 candies. If I asked for one half of his candies, how many candies did I want? *Ans:* 4 candies.

13. If out of 12 toys in the box half are cars, how many toy cars are in the box? *Ans:* 6 toys.

14. If out of 10 children in the class half are girls, how many girls are in the class? *Ans:* 5 girls.

15. Olga lit 6 birthday candles and blew out half. How many are still burning? *Ans:* 3 candles.

16. If one cat has 9 lives, how many lives do two cats have altogether? *Ans:* 18 lives.

17. Chris has 12 shoes. Half are for the left foot. How many are for the right?
    Ans: 6 shoes.

18. Half of 2 plus half of 4 is equal to what? *Ans:* 3.
    Solution: half of 2 is 1 and half of 4 is 2. Then, 1 + 2 = 3.

19. Half of 4 plus half of 10 equals to what? *Ans:* 7.
    Solution: half of 4 is 2 and half of 10 is 5. Then, 2 + 5 = 7.

20. Half of 10 plus half of 10 equals to what? *Ans:* 10.
    Solution: half of 10 is 5. Then, 5 + 5 = 10.

21. Half of 8 minus half of 8 equals to what? *Ans:* 0.
    Solution: half of 8 is equal 4. Then 4 - 4 = 0.

22. Half of 8 minus half of 4 equals to what? *Ans:* 2.
    Solution: half of 8 is 4 and half of 4 is 2. Then, 4 + 2 = 2.

Addition and subtraction with numbers up to 20

Exercise I

12 + 3 = 15	15 + 2 = 17	19 - 2 = 17	17 - 9 = 8
12 + 5 = 17	15 + 3 = 18	19 - 3 = 16	16 - 2 = 14
12 + 7 = 19	15 + 4 = 19	19 - 5 = 14	16 - 4 = 12
12 + 8 = 20	15 + 5 = 20	18 - 7 = 11	16 - 5 = 11
13 + 1 = 14	16 + 2 = 18	18 - 8 = 10	16 - 6 = 10
13 + 2 = 15	16 + 4 = 20	18 - 9 = 9	16 - 7 = 9
13 + 3 = 16	16 + 3 = 19	18 - 5 = 13	16 - 8 = 8
13 + 6 = 19	16 + 4 = 20	18 - 6 = 12	15 - 8 = 7
13 + 7 = 20	17 + 2 = 19	17 - 2 = 15	15 - 4 = 11
14 + 2 = 16	17 + 3 = 20	17 - 4 = 13	15 - 6 = 9
14 + 3 = 17	18 + 2 = 20	17 - 5 = 12	15 - 9 = 6
14 + 5 = 19	19 + 1 = 20	17 - 7 = 10	15 - 8 = 7
14 + 6 = 20	18 - 6 = 12	17 - 8 = 9	19 - 8 = 11

Exercise II

1 + 10 + 1 = 12	1 + 8 + 10 = 19	2 + 10 + 4 = 16	4 + 6 + 10 = 20
1 + 10 + 2 = 13	1 + 10 + 8 = 19	2 + 4 + 10 = 16	5 + 10 + 2 = 17
2 + 3 + 10 = 15	5 + 2 + 10 = 17	2 + 10 + 7 = 19	5 + 10 + 5 = 20
2 + 10 + 3 = 15	5 + 10 + 2 = 17	2 + 7 + 10 = 19	3 + 5 + 10 = 18
1 + 10 + 6 = 17	4 + 2 + 10 = 16	4 + 10 + 4 = 18	3 + 10 + 5 = 18
1 + 6 + 10 = 17	4 + 10 + 2 = 16	4 + 10 + 6 = 20	7 + 2 + 10 = 19

Word Problems

1. There are 7 runners on one team and 9 runners on another. How many runners are on both teams? *Ans:* 16 runners.
    a) If 8 runners competed in the first race, how many raced in the second? *Ans:* 8 runners.

2. For his birthday, Michael received $19. First, he spent $7 and then $7 more. How much does he have now? *Ans:* $5.

3.   Ali rode his bicycle uphill for 8 miles, then downhill for 12 miles. How many miles did he ride? *Ans:* 20 miles.

4.   I saved $12 and my mom gave me $5. How much money do I have now? *Ans:* $17.
    a) If I spent $13 at a music store. How much money is left? *Ans:* $4.

5.   Rolando had 12 crayons and bought 7 more. How many crayons does he have? *Ans:* 19 crayons.
    a) He broke 6. How many crayons does he have now? *Ans:* 13 crayons.

6.   Timmy earned 9 good-behavior-stars last week and 7 stars this week. But then he lost 10 stars for fighting. How many stars does he still have? *Ans:* 6 stars ($9 + 7 = 16$. Then, $16 - 10 = 6$).

7.   A mail carrier had 20 letters. He delivered 14 letters to the first house, 3 letters to the second house and 2 letters to the last house on the street. How many letters does he still have?
Ans: 1 letter, don't get tricked by the word last.

8.   Lucy had some candies. After she gave away 12 and ate 5, she had none left. How many candies did she start with? *Ans:* 17 candies.

9.   When the school year started a teacher had some notebooks. He used 6, lost 4 and still had 10 left at the end. How many notebooks did teacher have in the beginning? *Ans:* 20 notebooks.
Solution: 6 used notebooks + 4 lost notebooks + 10 left at the end notebooks = 20 notebooks.

10. There were 6 markers in the box before Tom put in 9 more. But when he checked again, there were only 11 markers in the box. How many markers are missing? *Ans:* 4 markers.
Solution: There were 6 markers + 9 markers Tom added to the box = 15 markers. Then, 15 markers (that were in the box) - 11 (are now in the box) = 4 markers are missing.

11. There were 9 dancers on the stage and then 9 more joined them. How many dancers are on the stage now? *Ans:* 18 dancers.

12. There were 18 mats in the room. Olga moved 6 to a storage room and the children took another 8. How many mats were left?
Ans: 4 mats ($18 - 6 = 12$, then $12 - 8 = 4$).

13. After the family took 9 pieces of wood from the firewood rack, there were 11 pieces left. How many pieces of wood were on the rack in the beginning? *Ans:* 20 pieces of wood.

14. Xenia had 9 apples and Irma brought 9 more apples to make a pie. How many apples are there now? *Ans:* 18 apples.
    a) After baking, there were 7 apples left. How many apples were used for the pie? *Ans:* 11 apples.

15. Colin buys groceries. He spent $6 on bread, $4 on milk and $5 on cereal. He had $5 left after all purchases. How much money did he have to start with? *Ans:* $20 (6 + 4 + 5 + 5 = 20).

16. A pet shop received an order for 11 dog tags and 5 cat tags. Only 14 tags were picked up by the customers. How many tags are still in the store? *Ans:* 2 tags (11 + 5 = 16, 16 - 14 = 2).

17. There were 19 children on my old team. This year 7 players left and 5 new players came. How many children are on my team now? *Ans:* 17 children (19 - 7 = 12, 12 + 5 = 17).

18. Last year we bought 17 bats for the team. During game season, 8 bats broke but we got 10 new bats. How many bats does the team have now? *Ans:* 19 bats.

19. Our team played 9 games at home and 7 games away. We won 11 games and lost 5. How many of the games were ties? *Ans:* 0 games or none (9 + 7 = 16, and 11 + 5 = 16).

20. Stormy, the poodle, chased 11 squirrels, 3 birds, 1 raccoon and 4 cats. How many creatures did he chase altogether? *Ans:* 19 creatures.

21. There were 14 people in the store. Eight people left and 11 new customers came in. How many people are in the store now? *Ans:* 17 people (14 - 8 = 6, then 6 + 11 = 17).

22. There were 19 students in the room. Ten students left and 7 came in. How many students are in the room now? *Ans:* 16 students.

23. There were 14 pigeons in the park; 6 more pigeons flew in and then 8 pigeons flew away. How many pigeons are in the park now? *Ans:* 12 pigeons (14 + 6 = 20, 20 - 8 = 12).

24. There were 16 cats on a tin roof. Eight cats left and 11 new cats came. How many cats are on the tin roof? *Ans:* 19 cats.

25. There were 11 surfers on the beach. Five surfers came out of the ocean but 7 surfers went in. How many surfers are on the beach now? *Ans:* 9 surfers (11 + 5= 16, 16 - 7 = 9).

26. There were 4 snakes in the snake pit. Thirteen more snakes slithered in and 9 snakes crawled out. How many snakes are in the pit now?
Ans: 8 snakes.

27. There were 7 ladybugs on the bush. Then 7 more flew in and 10 flew away. How many ladybugs are on the bush now? *Ans:* 4 ladybugs.

28. Tracy took out 4 marbles from her left pocket and 4 marbles from her right pocket and put them all on the table. Nick took out 4 marbles from his left pocket and 4 marbles from his right pocket and also put them all on the table. How many marbles are on the table? *Ans:* 16 marbles.

29. A soccer team won 12 games and lost 5. How many games did the team tie if it played 20 games this season? *Ans:* 3 games.

    Solution: 12 games won + 5 lost games = 17 games. 20 season games - 17 games (won and lost combined) = 3 games in a tie.

30. Paloma's mother had 6 eggs in one carton and double that amount in the other. She used 11 eggs to make an omelet. How many are left?
Ans: 7 eggs.

    Solution: One carton has 6 eggs. The other carton has double that, or 12 eggs. Both cartons have 6 + 12 = 18 eggs. Then 18 eggs - 11 eggs for the omelet = 7 eggs.

31. Hannah went to buy a cake. She took out two $10 bills, but the cake costs only $11. How much change will she bring back? *Ans:* $9.

32. If Hannah set the table for 14 people but only 9 came for the tea party, how many empty seats were there? *Ans:* 5 empty seats.

33. Harry can walk to school in 18 minutes. But when he is late, he runs there in 11 minutes. How many minutes does he save by running?
Ans: 7 minutes.

34. The pony's tail is 16 inches long and the donkey's tail is 9 inches long. By how much longer is the pony's tail than donkey's? *Ans:* 7 inches.

35. A small restaurant had to wash 5 glasses after lunch and 13 after dinner. After they washed 9, how many are left to be done?
Ans: 9 glasses (5 + 13 = 18, 18 - 9 = 9).

36. Hannah poured 20 ounces of milk into a bowl that holds 14 ounces. How many ounces of milk spilled over? *Ans:* 6 ounces.

37. There are always 16 chairs in the room. The family only uses 8 at breakfast time. How many chairs are empty at breakfast? *Ans:* 8 chairs.

38. How many colored pencils did Harry have after he lost 12 from the 20-pencil set he got for his birthday?
    Ans: 8 pencils. Harry must be more careful.

39. Sarah invited 16 friends to her party, but only 14 came. How many did not come? *Ans:* 2 friends.

40. A theater coatcheck room kept 7 coats and 9 jackets. After the show, there were still 4 jackets left in the room. How many coats and jackets were picked up? *Ans:* 12 coats and jackets.

41. For a party, Sarah baked 16 muffins; 13 were eaten. How many were not? *Ans:* 3 muffins.

42. What is the difference between Frank's age and Sarah's age if Frank is 8 years old and Sarah is 16? *Ans:* 8 years.

43. Dahlia has $12 in the bank and $6 in her purse. She took out $9 for a birthday present for her mother. How much does she have left? *Ans:* $9.

    Solution: $12 from the bank + $6 from the purse = $18.
    Then $18 - $9 for the present = $9 left.

44. Logan's duty is to wipe 18 desks in the classroom. He wiped 7 desks before the break and 7 desks after the break. How many desks are left to be wiped? *Ans:* 4 desks.

    Solution 1: There are 18 desks and Logan wiped 7 before the break, 18 - 7 = 11 desks remained. After the break Logan wiped another 7 desks, 11 - 7 = 4. The answer is 4.

    Solution 2: Logan wiped 7 desks before the break and 7 after, 7 + 7 = 14. There are 18 desks in class and Logan wiped 14, 18 - 14 = 4.

45. Mother baked 17 pancakes. She gave some to the children and now there are 8 left. How many were eaten? *Ans:* 9 pancakes.

46. We ordered 17 balloons for the party. After the party there were 6 balloons left. How many popped? *Ans:* 11 balloons.

47. There were 7 rabbits in one pen and 8 rabbits in the other. How many rabbits were left after we bought 2 rabbits from each pen? *Ans:* 11 rabbits.

    Solution 1: There were 7 rabbits in one pen and we bought 2, 7 - 2 = 5. There were 8 rabbits in the other pen and we bought 2, 8 - 2 = 6. Then 5 + 6 = 11

    Solution 2: There were 7 rabbits in one pen and 8 in the other, 7 + 8 = 15 in both pens. We bought 2 rabbits from each, 2 + 2 = 4. Then 15 rabbits in both pens - 4 rabbits we bought = 11. Remember! You can only add together the same things, like rabbits to rabbits in this problem.

48. A toy has 17 parts. Three parts are big, 9 parts are round, and 5 parts are green. How many white parts are there? *Ans:* it's impossible to tell.

We can't solve this problem because even if we know that there are 5 green parts we don't know what other colors are in the toy. We can't guess because it would make a new, different problem. We simply say that we can't solve this problem with the facts given. In math it's very important to know what problems we can and can't solve.

49. Victor takes 20 minutes to do his homework. Today, he did it 9 minutes faster. How long did it take him to do his homework today?
Ans: 11 minutes

A Challenge

50. Every morning Nina has to make her bed. Last week she missed 3 days. This week she missed 2 days. How many times did she make her bed during the last 2 weeks? Remember, there are 7 days in a week.
Ans: 9 days.

Solution: 7 days + 7 days = 14 days in 2 weeks; 2 days + 3 days = 5 missed days. 14 days (two weeks) - 5 days (missed in two weeks together) = 9 days (the bed was made).

Adding and subtracting coins up to 20

Let's learn coins:
A 1 cent coin is called a penny.
A 5 cents coin is called a nickel.
A 10 cents coin is called a dime.

Exercise I

One nickel is 5 cents. Two nickels are how many cents? *Ans:* 10 cents
Two nickels are 10 cents. Three nickels are how many cents? *Ans:* 15 cents
Three nickels are 15 cents. Four nickels are how many cents? *Ans:* 20 cents
One dime is 10 cents. Two dimes are how many cents? *Ans:* 20 cents

Word Problems

1. A nickel is 5 cents and a dime is 10 cents. How much is 1 nickel and 1 dime together? *Ans:* 15 cents.

2. A nickel is 5 cents and a dime is 10 cents. How much are 2 dimes? *Ans:* 20 cents.

3. A nickel is 5 cents and a dime is 10 cents. How much are 3 nickels? *Ans:* 15 cents.

4. A nickel is 5 cents and a dime is 10 cents. How much is 1 dime, 1 nickel and 1 penny altogether? *Ans:* 16 cents.

5. A nickel is 5 cents and a penny is 1 cent. How much are 3 pennies and 2 nickels together? *Ans:* 13 cents.

6. I gave 2 dimes for a sticker and received a nickel back. How much was my sticker? *Ans:* 15 cents.

7. I paid 3 nickels for a candy that cost 12 cents. How much change will I receive? *Ans:* 3 cents.

8. I bought 2 stamps with 2 dimes. One stamp costs 14 cents.
    a) How much is the other stamp? *Ans:* 6 cents.
    b) How many nickels and pennies will you pay for a 6 cent stamp?
       Ans: One of each (1 nickel and 1 penny).

9. I paid 2 dimes for the stamps. Can I pay with 4 nickels instead? *Ans:* Yes.
    Solution: 5 + 5 + 5 + 5 = 20 cents. 10 + 10 also makes 20 cents.

10. Which is more?
    a) 1 nickel and 3 pennies or 1 dime?
       Ans: 1 dime, because 5 + 3 = 8 cents and 1 dime is 10 cents
    b) 1 dime and 4 pennies or 3 nickels? *Ans:* 3 nickels, because 1 dime + 4
       pennies = 14 cents, but 3 nickels: 5 + 5 + 5 = 15 cents.
    c) 1 dime and 1 nickel or 3 nickels? *Ans:* They are the same, 15 cents.

11. If I have 20 cents and give 1 nickel away, how much will I have?
    Ans: 15 cents.

12. If I have 20 cents and give 2 nickels away, how much will I have?
    Ans: 10 cents.

13. If I had 20 cents and gave 3 nickels away, how much would I have left?
    Ans: 5 cents.

14. If I had 20 cents and gave 4 nickels away, how much would I have left?
    Ans: Nothing or 0 cents.

15. One hot cross bun costs one cent. If Mr. Bumble paid one dime and
    received 4 cents back in change, how many buns did he buy?
    Ans: 6 buns. That was long time ago, no one would sell you a hot cross
    bun for a penny anymore. Alas!

16. How much is 1 penny, 1 nickel and one dime together?
    Ans: 16 cents (1 + 5 + 10 = 16).

More addition and subtraction with numbers up to 20

Problem Solving

What is 17 - 12 = ?

First Solution: Step 1: We can say that 12 equals 10 + 2.
Step 2: Then 17 - 12 would be the same as 17 - 10, then minus 2.
Step 3: 17 - 10 = 7; then, 7 - 2 = 5.
The answer: 17 - 12 = 5.

Second Solution: Step 1: 17 equals 10 + 7, 12 equals 10 + 2
In other words: From 10 and 7 we need to take away 10 and 2, respectively
Step 2: Taking away 10 from 10 is easy. That equals 0.
Step 3: Now we take 2 from 7, that is 7 - 2 = 5
Step 4: 0 + 5 = 5
The answer is 5.

Rule

Do you remember that two-digit number means that there is a digit in the ones place and a digit in the tens place? These are the numbers between 9 and 100. Numbers 17, 26, 55 and 70 are all two-digit numbers. Number 9 is a one-digit number and number 100 is a three-digit number.

To subtract a two-digit number from another two-digit number you can take away tens from tens and ones from ones separately and then add the results together.

Review

Let's review the place values. You might remember that place value tells us about the worth of each digit in a number. In two-digit numbers like 17, 20, or 88, the digit on the right tells us how many ones the number has. The digit on the left tells us how many tens. Then, the number 17 has 7 ones and 1 tens.

The number 20 has 0 ones but 2 tens. The number 20 is larger than 17, because 2 tens are more than 1 ten and 7 ones.

The number 88 has 8 ones and 8 tens.

Three-digit numbers have place values for ones on the right, for tens in the middle and for hundreds on the left.

You might ask why we need place value. Here is why: Sometimes we need to add 2 two-digit numbers, for example 16 and 13. To make it easy, we can separately add the tens, 10 + 10 = 20, and the ones, 6 + 3 = 9. Now we can put 20 and 9 together and the answer is 29.

We can also use place value to do subtractions. For example, 17 - 14 can be solved by taking away 1 in tens in 14 from 1 in tens in 17, that's 0 (zero). Now, we can take 4 ones from 7 ones, and that's 3. The answer is 17 - 14 = 3.

Now, you try it.

1 + 10 = 11	5 + 14 = 19	15 - 13 = 2	18 - 12 = 6
1 + 11 = 12	4 + 15 = 19	15 - 12 = 3	18 - 15 = 3
2 + 11 = 13	3 + 17 = 20	16 - 11 = 5	18 - 14 = 4
2 + 12 = 14	6 + 11 = 17	16 - 12 = 4	19 - 11 = 8
3 + 11 = 14	6 + 12 = 18	16 - 15 = 1	19 - 12 = 7
3 + 13 = 16	6 + 14 = 20	16 - 12 = 4	19 - 18 = 1
2 + 14 = 16	7 + 12 = 19	16 - 13 = 3	19 - 17 = 2
3 + 12 = 15	7 + 11 = 18	17 - 10 = 7	19 - 15 = 4
4 + 12 = 16	7 + 13 = 20	17 - 11 = 6	19 - 16 = 3
2 + 15 = 17	8 + 11 = 19	17 - 16 = 1	20 - 10 = 10
2 + 18 = 20	12 - 11 = 1	16 - 12 = 4	20 - 11 = 9
3 + 16 = 19	13 - 11 = 2	17 - 12 = 5	20 - 19 = 1
1 + 19 = 20	14 - 12 = 2	17 - 13 = 4	20 - 15 = 5
2 + 16 = 18	14 - 11 = 3	17 - 14 = 3	20 - 18 = 2
5 + 11 = 16	14 - 13 = 1	18 - 11 = 7	20 - 12 = 8
5 + 13 = 18	15 - 14 = 1	18 - 17 = 1	20 - 17 = 3
5 + 15 = 20	15 - 11 = 4	18 - 16 = 2	20 - 16 = 4

Word Problems

1. There are 12 cups of tea in the pot, and we drank 11. How many cups are in the pot now? *Ans:* 1 cup.

2. There were 16 pieces of cake, and the party ate 14 of them. How many pieces are left? *Ans:* 2 pieces.

3. A gallery had 12 pictures. Later, it added 7 new pictures. How many are there now? *Ans:* 19 pictures.
   a) Then, they removed 10. How many are now? *Ans:* 9 pictures.
   b) Then, they added 6 more. How many are there now? *Ans:* 15 pictures.

4. A car dealer received 20 new trucks and sold 12 in the first week. How many are still there? *Ans:* 8 trucks.

5. Together, there are 20 monkeys and apes in a zoo. Of these, 18 are monkeys and the rest are apes. How many apes are in the zoo? *Ans:* 2 apes.

6. Eighteen monkeys got bananas. Eleven monkeys shared their bananas with the apes. How many did not share? *Ans:* 7 monkeys.
    Solution: 18 monkeys (with bananas) - 11 monkeys (who shared) = 7 monkeys (who didn't share).

7. A singer received 20 messages total. Fifteen were voice messages and the rest were e-mails. How many e-mail messages did the singer receive? *Ans:* 5 messages.

8. The singer returned 18 of her 20 messages. How many were left unanswered? *Ans:* 2 messages.

9. Twenty children went on a field trip. Seventeen children brought their lunches from home, and the rest had to buy their lunches. How many children paid for their lunches? *Ans:* 3 children.

10. Out of 17 lunches, 14 children had turkey sandwiches. How many did not? *Ans:* 3 children.

11. If I had 20 darts and threw 14, how many darts do I still have? *Ans:* 6 darts.

12. Out of 20 pigeons in his hat, a magician set 13 free. How many are still in the hat? *Ans:* 7 pigeons.

13. Out of 13 pigeons that came out of the hat, only 11 came back to the magician. How many pigeons are still flying around? *Ans:* 2 pigeons.

14. A cargo train has 19 cars. Twelve cars are painted brown, and the rest are red. How many red cars are there? *Ans:* 7 cars.

15. An ice skater tried a jump 20 times but fell 16 times. How many times did she make the jump? *Ans:* 4 times.

16. The ice skater earned 18 medals. She hung 12 medals on the wall and put the rest in a box. How many medals are in the medal box? *Ans:* 6 medals.

17. During a game, an umpire called "ball" 5 times and "strike" 13 times. The coach said that only 18 of his calls were fair. How many calls did the coach think were unfair?
    Ans: 0 calls or none. Don't get tricked by the word "only."

18. On the road, a motorcyclist passed 6 trucks and 12 cars. How many vehicles did he pass? *Ans:* 18 vehicles.

19. The red team had 9 players and the blue team had 7. How many players played altogether in the game? *Ans:* 16 players.
    a) The next day, 8 players quit the game. How many players stayed? *Ans:* 8 players.

20. Jim paid $12 for one book and $8 for the other. How much did he pay for both? *Ans:* $20.
    a) If Jim then sold both books for $14, how much money did he lose? *Ans:* $6.

21. In his back yard, Andrew counted 15 spiders. Of the 15 spiders, 13 were black widow spiders. How many were not? *Ans:* 2 spiders. A black widow spider's bite can be poisonous, but only females are dangerous.

22. There are 4 drummers and 15 trumpet players in the school band. Only 16 players came to practice because the rest had the flu. How many musicians stayed home? *Ans:* 3 musicians (4 + 15 = 19, then 19 - 16 = 3).

23. In a 14-story building, the first 5 floors are offices and the rest are apartments. How many apartment floors are in the building? *Ans:* 9 floors.

24. There were 8 roller skaters and 7 bicyclers at the park. How many children were at the park? *Ans:* 15 children.
    a) Thirteen children went home at 6 pm. How many stayed behind? *Ans:* 2 children.

25. An artist made 6 oil paintings and 13 watercolors. How many paintings did he make in total? *Ans:* 19 paintings.
    a) If he sold 11 and gave away 1, how many did he keep? *Ans:* 7 paintings (19 - 11 = 8, then 8 - 1 = 7).

26. There were 20 minutes before the play started. Ingrid spent 6 minutes getting dressed and 6 minutes putting on make-up. How many minutes did she have left to walk to the stage? *Ans:* 8 minutes.

    Solution 1: 20 min (before the play) - 6 min (getting dressed) = 14 minutes left. Then, 14 minutes - 6 min (on make-up) = 8 minutes (for walking to the stage).

    Solution 2: 6 min (to get dressed) + 6 min (on make-up) = 12 min (on both). Then, 20 min (before the play) - 12 min (for both, getting dressed and make up) = 8 minutes (walking to the stage).

27. An architect had 19 days to design a house. She took 5 days to make a sketch and 12 days to draw a plan. How many days were left to finish the work? *Ans:* 2 days.

    Solution: 5 days to sketch + 12 days to draw = 17 days for all the work. Then, 19 - 17 = 2 days left.

28. One sailor tied 4 knots and another tied 16 knots. How many knots did they both tie altogether? *Ans:* 20 knots.
    a) If 6 knots came undone, how many stayed tight? *Ans:* 14 knots.

29. The road is 4 miles uphill and 13 miles downhill. How long is the road? *Ans:* 17 miles.
    a) After walking 14 miles, how many more are left? *Ans:* 3 miles.

30. Jack has $5 in singles, one $5 bill and one $10 bill. How much money does he have? *Ans:* $20 (5 + 5 + 10 = 20).

31. Jordan bought a pair of scissors for $6 and a stapler for $12. How much did they both cost? *Ans:* $18.
    a) How much change will Jordan receive from $20? *Ans:* $2.

32. In a bouquet of 19 flowers, there are 7 tulips and 7 daffodils. The rest are daisies. How many are daisies? *Ans:* 5 daisies.

33. Take the number 6, add another 6 and then add another six. How much did you get? *Ans:* 18.

34. Tien cut an 18-yard rope into three pieces. The first piece is 6 yards and the second is also 6 yards. How long is the third? *Ans:* 6 yards.

    Solution 1: 18 yards (the whole rope) - 6 yards (the first piece) - 6 yards (the second piece) = 6 yards (the third piece).

    Solution 2: 6 yards (the first piece) + 6 yards (the second piece) = 12 yards (two pieces). Then 18 yards (the whole rope) - 12 (two pieces) = 6 yards (the third piece).

35. Nicky had a 15-yard rope and cut it in three parts. The first piece was 5 yards and the second was also 5 yards. How long was the third? *Ans:* 5 yards.

36. Orin cut his 20-yard rope into three pieces. The first was 7 yards; the second also 7 yards. How long was the third? *Ans:* 6 yards.

37. A barbershop had 17 customers. Twelve asked for a haircut and the rest asked for a shave. How many asked for a shave? *Ans:* 5 customers.

38. Out of 18 fruits in a bowls, 6 are apples, 6 are pears and the rest are lemons. How many lemons are in the bowl? *Ans:* 6 lemons.

39. Out of 15 vegetables on a plate, 5 are potatoes, 5 are tomatoes and the rest are yams. How many yams are on the plate? *Ans:* 5 yams.

40. Out of 12 berries in a saucer, 4 are gooseberries, 4 are cranberries and the rest are blueberries. How many blueberries are there? *Ans:* 4 blueberries.

41. Instead of finishing 18 problems in one hour, a student has done only 9. How many more are left to do? *Ans:* 9 problems.

42. There are 18 miles between two towns. A traveler ran 2 miles, walked 8 miles and rode in a car for the rest. How long was the car ride? *Ans:* 8 miles.

43. A hungry explorer ate 4 bowls of soup, 4 pieces of pizza, 4 salads and 4 desserts. How many dishes did he eat? *Ans:* 16 dishes.

44. Jerry was tossing cherry pits in the garbage can. Out of 19 tosses, he missed 14 times. How many pits got into the can? *Ans:* 5. We hope he cleaned up the rest!

45. Out of 20 watermelons, a store sold only 14. How many were not sold? *Ans:* 6 watermelons.

46. Eighteen stories were written for a 16-page newspaper. The first 4 pages had 4 stories, the next 4 pages had 5 stories and the next 3 pages had 6 stories. How many stories were left for the last 5 pages? *Ans:* 3 stories. If you missed the answer the first time, please listen to the problem again and remember that we are counting the stories, not the pages.

47. Out of 16 ice cubes, Fay used 5 for lemonade, 5 for iced tea and 5 for juice. How many ice cubes were left? *Ans:* 1 ice cube.

48. After graduating from flying school, 7 pilots flew north, 7 flew south and the rest flew west. If there were 18 graduates, how many flew west? *Ans:* 4 pilots.

49. A scientist did 17 experiments. Of these experiments, 8 experiments came out good and 8 came out bad. How many experiments were neither good nor bad? *Ans:* 1 experiment.

50. Tricia drew 19 pictures for an art show but only 11 pictures were accepted. How many were rejected? *Ans:* 8 pictures.

51. There are 20 nuts in a bowl: 16 are walnuts and the rest are hazelnuts. How many hazelnuts are in the bowl? *Ans:* 4 hazelnuts.

52. Mrs. Clark ordered 16 windows for the house. Seven were small windows and the rest were large. How many large windows did she order? *Ans:* 9 large windows.

53. A library received 19 books. There were 6 children's books, 6 novels and the rest were mysteries. How many mysteries did the library get? *Ans:* 7 mysteries.

54. A park ranger marked 17 old trees for cutting. There were 5 oaks and 6 pines. The rest were fir trees. How many fir trees were to be cut? *Ans:* 6 fir trees.

Addition up to 25

Problem Solving

Problem: $17 + 5 = ?$
Solution: Step 1: We can say that 5 equals $3 + 2$,
                Step 2: Then $17 + 5$ would be the same as $17 + 3 + 2$
                Step 3: $17 + 3 = 20$, $20 + 2 = 22$
                The answer: $17 + 5 = 22$.

In this problem we broke number 5 into two parts. One to make it up to next number that ends with a "0" and the other part to add on top. Let's try again.

Problem: $8 + 15 = ?$
Solution: Step 1: It would be easier to break 8 into two parts: 5 and 3
                Step 2: Then $8 + 15$ equals $5 + 3 + 15$ or $5 + 15 + 3$.
                Remember, when adding numbers together, the order does not matter.
                Step 3: $5 + 15 = 20$, $20 + 3 = 23$
                The answer: $8 + 15 = 23$.

Exercise I

$18 + 2 = 20$	$14 + 6 = 20$	$3 + 7 + 10 = 20$	$7 + 13 = 20$
$2 + 3 = 5$	$6 + 3 = 9$	$3 + 17 = 20$	$7 + 14 = 21$
$18 + 2 + 3 = 23$	$14 + 6 + 3 = 23$	$3 + 17 + 1 = 21$	$7 + 15 = 22$
$18 + 5 = 23$	$14 + 9 = 23$	$3 + 18 = 21$	$7 + 18 = 25$
$17 + 3 = 20$	$15 + 5 = 20$	$5 + 15 = 20$	$9 + 11 = 20$
$3 + 4 = 7$	$5 + 5 = 10$	$5 + 15 + 2 = 22$	$9 + 11 + 3 = 23$
$17 + 3 + 4 = 24$	$15 + 5 + 5 = 25$	$5 + 17 = 22$	$9 + 15 = 24$
$17 + 7 = 24$	$15 + 10 = 25$	$5 + 10 + 1 = 16$	$9 + 14 = 23$

Exercise II

What number and 18 make 20?   *Ans:* 2
What number and 16 make 20?   *Ans:* 4
What number and 10 make 20?   *Ans:* 10

What number and 5 make 20?	*Ans:* 15		
What number and 8 make 20?	*Ans:* 12		
What number and 6 make 20?	*Ans:* 14		
What number and 3 make 20?	*Ans:* 17		
What number and 7 make 20?	*Ans:* 13		
What number and 12 make 20?	*Ans:* 8		
What number and 13 make 20?	*Ans:* 7		
What number and 9 make 20?	*Ans:* 11		
What number and 11 make 20?	*Ans:* 9		
What number and 14 make 20?	*Ans:* 6		
What number and 15 make 20?	*Ans:* 5		
What number and 17 make 20?	*Ans:* 3		
What number and 2 make 20?	*Ans:* 18		

Exercise III

10 + 10 = 20	18 + 2 = 20	15 + 6 = 21	19 + 3 = 22
20 + 3 = 23	18 + 3 = 21	15 + 7 = 22	19 + 4 = 23
10 + 11 = 21	17 + 4 = 21	19 + 3 = 22	19 + 5 = 24
10 + 9 = 19	17 + 5 = 22	14 + 10 = 24	19 + 6 = 25
12 + 10 = 22	16 + 5 = 21	18 + 4 = 22	14 + 7 = 21
15 + 10 = 25	14 + 6 = 20	18 + 5 = 23	18 + 5 = 23
17 + 3 = 20	14 + 5 = 19	17 + 5 = 22	19 + 5 = 24
18 + 1 = 19	14 + 7 = 21	17 + 6 = 23	22 + 3 = 25
16 + 3 = 19	7 + 7 + 7 = 21	18 + 6 = 24	12 + 9 = 21
16 + 4 = 20	13 + 7 = 20	18 + 7 = 25	13 + 9 = 22
15 + 5 = 20	13 + 6 = 19	17 + 7 = 24	15 + 9 = 24

Word Problems

1. There were 19 notebooks on the shelf. I added 2 more. How many notebooks are on the shelf now? *Ans:* 21 notebooks.

2. There are 18 bats in the cave. Three more bats came to visit. How many bats are in the cave now? *Ans:* 21 bats.

3. There are 18 holes on the golf course. A gopher dug 4 more. How many holes are there now? *Ans:* 22 holes.

4. Today is the 19th. My concert is in 3 days. What is the date of my concert? *Ans:* The 22nd.

5. Before a ranch bought 7 more ponies, it already had 15. How many ponies does the ranch have now? *Ans:* 22 ponies.

6. There are 18 students in my class. Next year, there will be 4 more. How many will be in my class then? *Ans:* 22 students.

7. Jill paid $19 for a skirt and $4 for a shirt. How much did she spend on both? *Ans:* $23.

8. There were 17 gallons of gasoline in the tank. Uncle Orin added 5 more. How many gallons are in the tank now? *Ans:* 22 gallons.

9. Liana picked up 17 acorns and 4 mushrooms. How many items did she pick up? *Ans:* 21 items.

10. Fiona is 14 years old. How old she will be in 2 years? *Ans:* 16 years old.
    a) In 4 years? *Ans:* 18 years old.
    b) In 5 years? *Ans:* 19 years old.
    c) In 6 years? *Ans:* 20 years old.
    d) In 8 years? *Ans:* 22 years old.

11. There were 16 penguins on the island. Five baby penguins hatched this month. How many penguins are on the island now? *Ans:* 21 penguins.

12. The teacher gave us 4 math problems in class and 17 to do at home. How many math problems did we get in total? *Ans:* 21 problems.

13. Yoram fed 6 nuts to his parakeet and 16 nuts to his parrot. How many nuts did he feed to his pets? *Ans:* 22 nuts.

14. Gail memorized 16 poems last month and 5 more this month. How many poems did she memorize? *Ans:* 21 poems.

15. Olaf can get across the lawn in 16 jumps and 7 cartwheels. How many movements does it take for Olaf to get across? *Ans:* 23 movements.

16. Mom wrote 18 checks last week and 5 checks this week. How many checks did mom write in 2 weeks? *Ans:* 23 checks.

17. Amy planted 17 cherry trees and 6 peach trees. How many trees did she plant in total? *Ans:* 23 trees:

18. There are $16 in my left pocket and $6 in my right pocket. How much money do I have altogether? *Ans:* $22.

19. After Aisha sold 4 tickets for the school concert, there were still 19 tickets left. How many tickets did she have in the beginning? *Ans:* 23 tickets.

20. There are 14 CDs in the box and 8 on the shelf. How many CDs are there in total? *Ans:* 22 CDs.

21. A broken clock struck 12 times and then 9 more times. How many times did the clock strike? *Ans:* 21 times.

22. Betsy drew 7 planets and 15 stars. How many heavenly bodies did she draw? *Ans:* 22 heavenly bodies.

23. There are 19 passengers and 4 crew members on a plane. How many people are on the plane altogether? *Ans:* 23 people.

24. The city zoo has 12 zebras and 9 giraffes. How many zebras and giraffes are in the zoo? *Ans:* 21 zebras and giraffes.

25. A coffee shop sold 9 muffins and 9 doughnuts. How many pastries did they sell? *Ans:* 18 pastries.

26. The team has 9 skiers and 11 snowboarders on the mountain. How many people are there? *Ans:* 20 people.

27. There are 12 motorcycles and 9 cars in the parking lot. How many vehicles are there? *Ans:* 21 vehicles.

28. It took a poet 13 days to write the words for a song. Then, it took a composer 10 days to write the music. How long did it take them to finish the song? *Ans:* 23 days.

29. I am inside an office in a tall building. There are 11 floors above me and 9 floors below. How many floors are in the building? *Ans:* 21 floors.

    Solution: It's tricky…11 + 9 = 20 floors, but there is also the floor where I am. Then, 20 + 1 = 21.

30. There are 14 miles to the rest stop on a bicycle course and another 9 to the finish. How many miles are in the course? *Ans:* 23 miles.

31. The big city fire department has 13 fire engines and 8 fire trucks (they are different). How many vehicles do they have? *Ans:* 21 vehicles.

32. I am reading a mystery book. Before school, I read 14 pages, and after school, I read 9 more. How many pages have I read? *Ans:* 23 pages.

33. Liz put 15 apples in a big basket and 8 apples in a small one. How many apples are in both baskets? *Ans:* 23 apples.

34. A newspaper printed 7 articles on one page and 16 articles on the other page. How many articles are on both pages? *Ans:* 23 articles.

35. The same newspaper printed 12 ads in the first section and 10 ads in the second section. How many ads do both sections have? *Ans:* 22 ads.

36. One pint is 16 ounces and one cup has 8 ounces. How many ounces do one pint and one cup make together? *Ans:* 24 ounces.

37. If Louis lifts 14 pounds with his right hand and 8 pounds with his left, how many pounds does he lift with both? *Ans:* 22 pounds.

38. Fourteen students joined the Guitar Club and 9 students joined the Ski Club. How many members are in both clubs? *Ans:* 23 members.

39. A toymaker made 6 tops and 16 whistles. How many toys did he make? *Ans:* 22 toys.

40. A hungry stork ate 7 frogs and 14 earthworms. How many creatures did the stork eat? *Ans:* 21 creatures.

41. The farmer's daughter collected 9 eggs from one coop and 15 from the other one. How many eggs did she collect? *Ans:* 24 eggs.

42. One of my books is 14 inches tall and the other is 11. How tall will they be if I put one on top of the other? *Ans:* 25 inches.

43. One farm has 11 acres; another farm has 10 acres. How many acres do they have together? *Ans:* 21 acres.

44. Kira, a gold fish, blew 13 bubbles. Mira, the guppy, blew 9. How many bubbles did they both blow? *Ans:* 22 bubbles.

45. The little doggy in the window costs $19 and the dog food costs $5. How much does the doggy and the dog food cost together? *Ans:* $24.

46. A box of candy had 16 dark chocolates and 8 milk chocolates. How many candies are in the box altogether? *Ans:* 24 candies.

47. Jenny's collection has 8 dolls with brown hair, 9 with blond hair and 1 doll with no hair at all. How many dolls does she have? *Ans:* 18 dolls.

48. Putting a picture on the board took 13 yellow pins and 8 red ones. How many pins did it take? *Ans:* 21 pins.

49. The car drove 19 miles and then 5 more. How many miles did it go? *Ans:* 24 miles.

50. A palace had 17 rooms and added 8 more rooms later. How many rooms are in the palace now? *Ans:* 25 rooms.

Adding equal numbers

Exercise I

Count forward from 0 to 30 by adding 2 (i.e., 2, 4, 6, 8, etc.)
Count forward from 0 to 30 by adding 3 (i.e., 3, 6, 9, 12, etc.)
Count forward from 0 to 28 by adding 4 (i.e., 4, 8, 12, etc.)
Count forward from 0 to 30 by adding 5 (i.e., 5, 10, 15, etc.)
Count forward from 0 to 30 by adding 6 (i.e., 6, 12, 18, etc.)
Count forward from 0 to 28 by adding 7 (i.e., 7, 14, 21, 28, etc.)
Count forward from 0 to 24 by adding 8 (i.e., 8, 16, 24.)
Count forward from 0 to 27 by adding 9 (i.e., 9, 18, and 27.)
Count forward from 0 to 30 by adding 10 (i.e., 10, 20, and 30.)
Count down from 30 to 0 by 2 (i.e., 30, 28, 26, 24, 22, etc.)
Count down from 30 to 0 by 3 (i.e., 30, 27, 24, 21, etc.)
Count down from 30 to 2 by 4 (i.e., 30, 26, 22, 18, etc.)
Count down from 30 to 0 by 5 (i.e., 30, 25, 20, 15, etc.)
Count down from 30 to 0 by 6 (i.e., 30, 24, 18, etc.)
Count down from 30 by 7 (i.e., 30, 23, 16, 9, 2.)
Count down from 30 by 8 (i.e., 30, 22, 14, etc.)
Count down from 29 by 8 (i.e., 29, 21, 13, 5.)
Count down from 30 by 9 (i.e., 30, 21, 12, 3.)
Count down from 30 by 10.

Exercise II

1 + 1 = 2	8 + 8 = 16	15 + 15 = 30	11 + 11 = 22
2 + 2 = 4	9 + 9 = 18	9 + 9 = 18	12 + 12 = 24
3 + 3 = 6	10 + 10 = 20	8 + 8 = 16	7 + 7 = 14
4 + 4 = 8	11 + 11 = 22	7 + 7 = 14	6 + 6 = 12
5 + 5 = 10	12 + 12 = 24	7 + 7 = 14	3 + 3 = 6
6 + 6 = 12	13 + 13 = 26	5 + 5 = 10	5 + 5 = 10
7 + 7 = 14	14 + 14 = 28	10 + 10 = 20	2 + 2 = 4

Exercise III

1 + 1 + 1 = 3	5 + 5 + 5 = 15	2 + 2 + 2 + 2 = 8
3 + 3 + 3 = 9	6 + 6 + 6 = 18	3 + 3 + 3 + 3 = 12
2 + 2 + 2 = 6	7 + 7 + 7 = 21	4 + 4 + 4 + 4 = 16
4 + 4 + 4 = 12	8 + 8 + 8 = 24	5 + 5 + 5 + 5 = 20

Exercise IV

11 + 15 = 26	12 + 16 = 28	17 + 12 = 29	12 + 18 = 30
12 + 11 = 23	12 + 17 = 29	14 + 14 = 28	15 + 14 = 29
13 + 12 = 25	11 + 17 = 28	13 + 13 = 26	17 + 13 = 30
15 + 12 = 27	13 + 11 = 24	18 + 11 = 29	14 + 16 = 30
15 + 13 = 28	16 + 12 = 28	11 + 19 = 30	20 + 10 = 30

Word Problems

1. Erin has 3 red balloons, 3 green balloons and 3 blue balloons. How many balloons does she have? *Ans:* 9 balloons.

2. I bought 4 pencils, 4 pens and 4 crayons. How many writing tools did I get? *Ans:* 12 tools.

3. Jack, John and Josh have $5 each. How much money do they have together? *Ans:* $15.

4. A king sent 4 knights to the west, 4 knights to the north, 4 knights to the east and 4 knights to the south. How many knights did he send away? *Ans:* 16 knights.

5. There are 5 players on each basketball team. How many players are on 2 basketball teams? *Ans:* 10 players.
    a) On 3 basketball teams? *Ans:* 15 players.
    b) On 4 basketball teams? *Ans:* 20 players.

6. There are 6 players on each hockey team. How many players are on 2 hockey teams? *Ans:* 12 players.
    a) On 3 hockey teams? *Ans:* 18 players.
    b) On 4 hockey teams? *Ans:* 24 players.

7. There are 7 players in a game. How many players are in 2 games? *Ans:* 14 players.
    a) In 3 games? *Ans:* 21 players.

8. A spider has 8 legs. How many legs do 2 spiders have altogether?
Ans: 16 legs.
a) 3 spiders? *Ans:* 24 legs.

9. Grace took 11 steps forward and 11 steps backward. How many steps did she take altogether? *Ans:* 22 steps.

10. Keith holds 12 ladybugs on his right hand and 12 ladybugs on his left. How many does he hold in both hands? *Ans:* 24 ladybugs.

11. There are 10 seats in the first row and 10 seats in the second. How many seats are in both rows? *Ans:* 20 seats.

12. There are 9 chickens in one coop and 9 in the other one. How many chickens are in both coops? *Ans:* 18 chickens.

13. If one cube has 6 sides, how many sides do 2 cubes have? *Ans:* 12 sides.

14. If it takes 8 minutes to wash one window, how much time does it take to wash two? *Ans:* 16 minutes.

15. One necklace costs $7. How much do 2 necklaces cost? *Ans:* $14.

16. It takes one hour to plant 6 rose bushes. How many rose bushes can we plant in 2 hours? *Ans:* 12 rose bushes.

17. It took a runner 8 minutes to run the first mile and 8 minutes to run the second mile. How much time did it take her to run 2 miles?
Ans: 16 minutes.
a) If she keeps running at the same pace, how much time will it take her to run 3 miles? *Ans:* 24 minutes.

18. For the school dance, 11 girls invited 11 boys. How many pairs were dancing? *Ans:* 11 pairs.

    Solution: Tricked you again! A pair means two. One boy and one girl make one pair.
    Let's try again: 11 boys invited 11 girls. How many kids were dancing?
    Ans: 22 kids. Correct!

19. I counted 12 teeth on top and 12 on the bottom in my sister's mouth. How many teeth does she have? *Ans:* 24 teeth.

20. My guitar has 6 strings. How many strings will 2 guitars have in total?
Ans: 12 strings.
a) How many strings will 3 guitars have in total? *Ans:* 18 strings.

21. If one CD has 7 songs, how many songs do 2 CDs have? *Ans:* 14 songs.
a) How many songs do 3 CDs have? *Ans:* 21 songs.

22. Neil made 6 paper planes, Olga made 6, and Paul also made 6. How many paper planes did all three make? *Ans:* 18 planes.

23. It took Kelly 8 days on a train, 8 days on a boat and 8 days on the bus to get home. How many days did she travel? *Ans:* 24 days.

24. A clown, who is 6 feet tall, wears a 6 foot tall hat. How tall is the clown from his toes to the top of his hat? *Ans:* 12 feet.

25. There are 11 players on one soccer team and 11 on the other team. How many players are on both teams combined? *Ans:* 22 players.

26. Henry put 12 eggs in a basket and then added 12 more eggs to the same basket. The basket fell and all the eggs broke. How many eggs broke? *Ans:* 24 eggs. Don't put all your eggs in one basket.

27. In a day, there are 12 hours before noon and 12 hours after. How many hours are in a whole day? *Ans:* 24 hours.

28. If a farm has 14 sheep and 14 horses, how many animals does it have altogether? *Ans:* 28 animals.

29. Georgie Porgie kissed 8 girls and made them cry. Then, 8 girls kissed him back and made him cry. How many kisses were exchanged? *Ans:* 16 kisses (8 + 8 = 16).

30. If one dog weighs 15 pounds and another weighs 11 pounds, how much do they both weigh? *Ans:* 26 pounds.

31. Two women went shopping and each spent $15. How much did they both spend? *Ans:* $30.

32. Mr. Roberts took a taxi to the station for 7 miles and then a train to town for 20 miles. How far did he travel? *Ans:* 27 miles.

33. Mrs. Roberts's grandma lives 13 miles from her home. How many miles is the round trip to grandma's house? *Ans:* 26 miles.

    Solution: Round trip means going to the place and coming back; then 13 miles + 13 miles = 26 miles.

34. Our team scored 9 goals, but the other team tied the game. How many goals were scored in the game in total? *Ans:* 18 goals.

35. A contractor builds 12 feet of a fence. Then he took some time off and came back to build 13 feet more. How many feet of fence did he build from start to finish? *Ans:* 25 feet.

36. Judy was making a dog run. She made it 19 feet long, but then decided to add 7 more feet. How long is the dog run now? *Ans:* 26 feet.

37. A rope was cut into three equal parts. Each part is 10 feet. How long was the rope initially? *Ans:* 30 feet (10 + 10 + 10 = 30).

38. A different rope was cut into 4 equal parts and each part was 6 feet. How long was the rope initially? *Ans:* 24 feet.

39. There are 16 students in one class and 13 students in the other class. How many students are in both classes? *Ans:* 29 students.

40. Ann has 12 game points, and Bob has 18. How many points do they both have altogether? *Ans:* 30.

41. I picked 7 flowers on Tuesday and 18 flowers on Wednesday. How many flowers did I pick on both days? *Ans:* 25 flowers.

42. The first clown threw 14 pies and another clown threw 14 pies back. How many pies did they both throw? *Ans:* 28 pies.

43. The giant's head and neck is 6 feet, his trunk is 10 feet and his legs are 11 feet long. How tall is the giant?
Ans: 27 feet (6 + 10 = 16, then 16 + 11 = 27).

44. A little boy weighs 13 pounds and his twin sister is 15 pounds. How much do both weigh? *Ans:* 28 pounds.

45. Grace spent 13 cents on an envelope and 13 cents on a stamp. How much money did she spend? *Ans:* 26 cents.

46. I counted 15 red flags, 6 green ones and 7 purple ones. How many flags did I count altogether? *Ans:* 28 flags.

47. The class has 13 girls and 17 boys. How many children are in the class altogether? *Ans:* 30 children.

48. In a small town parade, there were 12 soldiers, 8 Marines and 8 Coast Guards. How many people participated in the parade?
Ans: 28 people.

49. To solve the first 15 math problems, a student used a calculator. For the other 7 problems, she did not. How many problems did she solve altogether? *Ans:* 22 problems.

50. A horse galloped 9 miles and walked 18. How many miles did it go?
Ans: 27 miles.

51. "How much is this puppy in the window?" asked little Tommy. "It would be $18 plus $7 for the basket," said the store owner. How much will Tommy have to pay altogether? *Ans:* $25.

52. There are 7 bones, called vertebrae, in the neck, 12 in the chest and 5 in the lower back. How many vertebrae are in the neck, chest and lower back altogether? *Ans:* 24 vertebrae.

53. At a party, 14 guests had coffee and 9 had tea. How many drinks were served? *Ans:* 23 drinks.

54. Imagine you are swimming in the ocean. First, 9 sharks come and then 12 more sharks come and start circling around you. Then, 5 new hungry sharks come. What should you do?
Ans: Stop imagining and you'll be OK.

Subtracting numbers
up to 25

Exercise I

Count backward from 25 to 0 by 1 (i.e., 25, 24, 23)
Count backward from 25 to 0 by 2 (i.e., 25, 23, 21)
Count backward from 25 by 3 (i.e., 25, 22, 19, 16)
Count backward from 25 by 4 (i.e., 25, 21, 17, 13, 9, 5, 1)
Count backward from 25 by 5 (i.e., 25, 20, 15, 10, 5, 0)
Count backward from 25 by 6 (i.e., 25, 19, 13, 7, 1)
Count backward from 25 by 7 (i.e., 25, 18, 11, 4)
Count backward from 25 by 8 (i.e., 25, 17, 9, 1)

Problem: 25 - 7 = ?
Solution: Step 1: 7 is made of 5 and 2.
Step 2: We can change the problem to 25 - 5, and from what is left, take away 2.
Step 3: 25 - 5 = 20. Then, 20 - 2 = 18.
Therefore, 25 - 7 = 18.

Problem: 25 - 11 = ?
Solution: Step 1: 11 is 10 + 1.
Step 2: From 25, we will take away 10 and then 1.
Step 3: 25 - 10 = 15. Then, 15 - 1 = 14.
Therefore 25 - 11 = 14.

Exercise II

2 + 3 = 5	4 + 4 = 8	6 + 3 = 9	1 + 7 = 8
22 - 2 = 20	24 - 4 = 20	26 - 6 = 20	21 - 1 = 20
20 - 3 = 17	20 - 4 = 16	20 - 3 = 17	20 - 7 = 13
22 - 5 = 17	24 - 8 = 16	26 - 9 = 17	21 - 8 = 13

Exercise III

25 - 10 = 15	15 - 10 = 5	13 - 5 = 8	23 - 11 = 12
25 - 11 = 14	22 - 7 = 15	23 - 5 = 18	24 - 13 = 11
25 - 12 = 13	15 - 6 = 9	23 - 7 = 16	22 - 9 = 13
25 - 13 = 12	25 - 16 = 9	23 - 17 = 6	22 - 18 = 4
15 - 14 = 1	25 - 6 = 19	20 - 12 = 8	23 - 11 = 12
25 - 14 = 11	25 - 21 = 4	23 - 9 = 14	22 - 19 = 3
25 - 13 = 12	23 - 9 = 14	23 - 7 = 16	13 - 9 = 4
25 - 15 = 10	22 - 11 = 11	23 - 13 = 10	22 - 9 = 13
15 - 15 = 0	24 - 9 = 15	23 - 12 = 11	13 - 7 = 6
25 - 6 = 19	21 - 6 = 15	23 - 19 = 4	22 - 7 = 15
15 - 7 = 8	24 - 9 = 15	13 - 9 = 4	11 - 2 = 9
25 - 7 = 18	24 - 11 = 13	23 - 7 = 16	21 - 2 = 19
25 - 9 = 16	24 - 14 = 10	23 - 14 = 9	11 - 4 = 7
15 - 8 = 7	24 - 8 = 16	22 - 12 = 10	21 - 4 = 17
24 - 8 = 16	24 - 14 = 10	22 - 8 = 14	11 - 5 = 6
15 - 9 = 6	21 - 19 = 2	22 - 11 = 11	11 - 6 = 5
25 - 9 = 16	24 - 21 = 3	13 - 11 = 2	21 - 5 = 16

Exercise IV

1. Two numbers added together equal 21. If one of the numbers is 10, what is the other one? *Ans:* 11.

2. Two numbers added together equal 29. If one of the numbers is 10, what is the other one? *Ans:* 19.

3. Two numbers added together equal 23. If one of the numbers is 11, what is the other one? *Ans:* 12.

4. Two numbers added together equal 23. If one of the numbers is 10, what is the other one? *Ans:* 13.

5. Two numbers added together equal 22. If one of the numbers is 11, what is the other one? *Ans:* 11.

6. Two numbers added together equal 24. If one of the numbers is 12, what is the other one? *Ans:* 12.

7. Two numbers added together equal 28. If one of the numbers is 17, what is the other one? *Ans:* 11.

8. Two numbers added together equal 24. If one of the numbers is 13, what is the other one? *Ans:* 11.

9. Two numbers added together equal 27. If one of the numbers is 13, what is the other one? *Ans:* 14.

10. Two numbers added together equal 28. If one of the numbers is 16, what is the other one? *Ans:* 12.

11. Two numbers added together equal 26. If one of the numbers is 19, what is the other one? *Ans:* 7.

12. Two numbers added together equal 24. If one of the numbers is 5, what is the other one? *Ans:* 19.

13. Two numbers added together equal 23. If one of the numbers is 13, whatis the other one? *Ans:* 10.

Learning a trick
Subtracting 19 from a two digit number: 25 - 19 = ?
   Solution: Step 1: Let's pretend that instead of 19,
                 we subtract 20 from 25.
                 Then, 25 - 20 = 5. Easy!
                 Step 2: But we took away 20 which is bigger than 19 by 1.
                 Now we need to give it back. 5 + 1 = 6.
                 25 - 19 = 6.

Word Problems

1. One dozen is 12. How many is 2 dozen? *Ans:* 24.

2. The story is 20 pages long. I have read 7 pages. How many pages are left to read? *Ans:* 13 pages.

3. This story has 22 pages. I read 4. How many are left to read? *Ans:* 18 pages.

4. There are 24 hours in a day. If you sleep 10 hours, how many hours will you be awake? *Ans:* 14 hours.
   a) If you sleep 8 hours, how many hours are you awake? *Ans:* 16 hours.
   b) If grandpa sleeps only 6 hours, how many hours is he awake?
   Ans: 18 hours.

5. Out of 24 students in a class, 14 cleaned the yard and the rest cleaned the classroom. How many stayed to clean the classroom? *Ans:* 10 students.

6. There were 25 chocolate candies in the box. Steve ate 6. How many are left? *Ans:* 19 candies.

6. There were 25 chocolate candies in the box. Steve ate 6. How many are left? *Ans:* 19 candies.

7. There were 21 boats on the lake at 1 o'clock in the afternoon. At 3 o'clock, there were only 12. How many boats left after 1 o'clock? *Ans:* 9 boats.

8. There are 7 birds in the cage and 21 in the bush. How many more birds are in the bush? *Ans:* 14 birds.

9. There are 5 rangers in the park and 17 campers. How many people are in the park total? *Ans:* 22 people.

10. At the age of 22, Jordan will finish his service in the army. He is 19 years old now. How many more years are left for him to serve? *Ans:* 3 years.

11. Olga received 24 letters and opened 19. How many more letters are left to be opened? *Ans:* 5 letters.

12. Out of 21 students on the gymnastics team, 9 are boys. How many girls are on the team?
    Ans: 12 girls. Remember the "subtracting 9 from a number" trick?

13. Corbin's jacket has 15 pockets. He filled 8 pockets with stuff. How many pockets are empty? *Ans:* 7 pockets.

14. Trish scored 24 points in a game. Sam scored 7. How many points separate them? *Ans:* 17 points.

15. Gaston bought a beret and a scarf for $21. The scarf was $5. How much was the beret? *Ans:* $16.

16. My sister is 8 years old. My age added to hers equals 21. How old am I? *Ans:* 13 years old.

17. I am 15. My age added to my cousin's age equals 23. How old is my cousin? *Ans:* 8 years old.

18. A canary and a cage cost $25 in total. The canary costs $8. How much is the cage? *Ans:* $17.

19. There are 21 mail boxes on Kim's street. She wants to invite everyone on her street to her barbeque. She put invitations in 10 mailboxes. How many are left? *Ans:* 11 mail boxes.

20. A rental store had 23 bicycles. They rented 9 bikes. How many bikes are still in the store? *Ans:* 14 bikes.

21. If 7 geese join 18 ducks, how many birds will swim on the lake?
    Ans: 25 birds.

22. Don saw 25 peaches in the pantry. He took 7 for a pie. How many are left? *Ans:* 18 peaches.

23. A squirrel gathered 24 grapes and ate 13 right away. She saved the rest to make raisins. How many raisins will she make? *Ans:* 11 raisins.

24. A carton has 24 ounces of milk. Dave poured 8 ounces into a glass. How many ounces are left in the carton? *Ans:* 16 ounces.

25. Phil bought 25 cupcakes and asked the baker to cut 10 of them in half. How many cupcakes were uncut? *Ans:* 15 cupcakes.

26. Fiona can do a handstand for 21 seconds, which is 10 seconds longer than Carla is able. How long can Carla stay on her hands? *Ans:* 11 seconds.

27. A sailboat reached Hawaii in 23 days. On the way back, it took 7 days less. How many days did the trip back last? *Ans:* 16 days.

28. How much are two dozen?
    Ans: 24. Remember that the other name for 12 is one dozen.

29. Two dozen is 24. One dozen is 12, how much is the other dozen?
    Ans: 12. Ha-ha, it is also 12, because any dozen is always 12.

30. My dog weighs 19 pounds, and my cat weighs 10 pounds.
    a) By how many pounds is the cat lighter than the dog? *Ans:* 9 pounds.
    b) How much do they weigh together?
       Ans: 29 pounds. That wasn't hard, was it?

31. Two boys together caught 24 trout. The first boy caught 12. How many did the second boy catch? *Ans:* 12 trout.

32. It takes 25 minutes to row the boat up the stream and only 10 minutes to row gently down the stream. By how much is the downstream trip shorter? *Ans:* 15 minutes.

33. There are 25 steps from the bottom of the stairs to the top. A puppy climbed 9 steps. How many steps remain to the top? *Ans:* 16 steps.

34. There were 23 rabbits in the meadow. When a dog barked, 11 rabbits ran. When an eagle flew over, another 8 took off. How many brave rabbits stayed in the meadow? *Ans:* 4 rabbits.

35. A doctor ordered 25 flu shots. The nurse gave 9 shots today. How many shots are left for tomorrow? *Ans:* 16 shots.

36. Two rocks together weigh 21 pounds. One rock weighs 9 pounds. How much does the other rock weigh? *Ans:* 12 pounds.

37. I paid $25 and received change of $6. How much did I spend? *Ans:* $19.

38. There were 22 blueberries on Valerie's plate. She ate 9 and her pet monkey ate 13. How many berries are still on the plate?
Ans: 0 berries or none.

39. Goofy had 20 math homework problems. He did 8 of them wrong and forgot to do 5. How many problems did Goofy solve correctly?
Ans: 7 problems (20 - 5 - 8 = 7).

40. There are 24 houses on Kiki's street. There are 12 houses on one side of the street. How many are on the other side? *Ans:* 12 houses.

41. There are 24 hours in a day.
   a) If a doctor worked for 12 hours, how much time did he rest?
      Ans: 12 hours.
   b) If a nurse worked 10 hours, how much time did she have off?
      Ans: 14 hours.
   c) If an ambulance driver worked 11 hours, how many hours did he have to rest? *Ans:* 13 hours.
   d) If a security guard worked 16 hours, how much time off did he have?
      Ans: 8 hours.

42. Sleepy can sleep 16 hours a day. Today, he slept 9 hours. How many hours did he stay awake? *Ans:* 15 hours.

   Solution: There are 24 hours in a day. Sleepy slept 9 hours. 24 - 9 = 15 hours. Don't get confused by 16 hours Sleepy can sleep. Knowing that doesn't help to solve the problem.

43. Sneezy always sneezes 23 times. He sneezed 7 times so far. How many more times he will sneeze? *Ans:* 16 times.

44. Grumpy grumped 17 times and then 6 times more. How many grumps did he do? *Ans:* 23 grumps.

45. Doc put 23 pills in a bottle and then took 12 pills out. How many pills are in the bottle now? *Ans:* 11 pills.

46. Marisa received 23 presents for her birthday. She already sent 9 "Thank you" cards. How many cards does she still need to send? *Ans:* 14 cards.

47. There are 24 problems on the math test. Ethan has finished 7. How many more are left to do? *Ans:* 17 problems.

48. There were 23 apples on the tree. We picked some and now there are 5 apples left. How many did we pick? *Ans:* 18 apples.

49. Lucas washed 22 shirts for the whole rugby team. He gave out 11 shirts for today's game and put away the rest. How many did he put away?
Ans: 11 shirts.

50. Holly took 24 pictures with her new camera, but only 19 pictures came out well. How many pictures came out bad? *Ans:* 5 pictures.

51. The birdwatchers spotted 19 birds. They saw 8 hummingbirds, 7 mockingbirds and the rest were woodpeckers. How many woodpeckers did they see? *Ans:* 4 woodpeckers.

52. Twenty-five cars were racing, but only 12 cars came to the finish line. How many dropped out of the race? *Ans:* 13 cars.

53. A nurse gave 16 shots. Seven shots were for chicken pox and the rest for measles. How many measles shot did she give? *Ans:* 9 shots.

Subtracting single and double-digit numbers up to 30

Problem: 27 - 13 = ?

First Solution: Step 1: 13 is 10 + 3

Step 2: From 27, we will take away 10 first, then subtract 3 more.

27 - 10 = 17 and 17 - 3 = 14

Therefore, 27 - 13 = 14.

Second Solution: Step 1: We will break the numbers into tens and ones.

27 = 2 tens (or 20) and 7 ones

13 = 1 of tens (or 10) and 3 ones

Step 2: We will take away tens from tens and ones from ones.

20 - 10 = 10 and 7 - 3 = 4

Step 3: Let's put tens and ones back together.

10 + 4 = 14

Then 27 - 13 = 14.

Problem: 30 - 18 = ?

First Solution: Step 1: 18 is 10 + 8

Step 2: From 30, we will take away 10 first, and then take away another 8.

30 - 10 = 20 and 20 - 8 = 12

Therefore, 30 - 18 = 12.

Second Solution: Step 1: We will break the numbers into tens and ones.

30 = 3 tens (or 20) and 0 ones

18 = 1 tens (or 10) and 8 ones

Step 2: We will take away tens from tens and ones from ones.

30 - 10 = 20 and 0 - 3 = ...

Wait a second, we don't know how to take 3 from zero.

We don't know yet how to take something from nothing.

Let's try again

Step 1: Let's break 30 in to 20 and 10 or 2 tens and 10 ones. Right?

Step 2: Now, we will take 10 from 20, 20 - 10 = 10

Then, take 8 from 10, 10 - 8 = 2.

Step 3: 10 + 2 = 12

30 - 18 = 12.

Exercise I

2 + 10 = 12	21 - 16 = 5	25 - 8 = 17	28 - 11 = 17
22 - 2 = 20	25 - 9 = 16	25 - 7 = 18	28 - 12 = 16
20 - 10 = 10	21 - 11 = 10	22 - 3 = 19	28 - 18 = 10
22 - 12 = 10	28 - 18 = 10	22 - 6 = 16	28 - 17 = 11
3 + 10 = 13	28 - 17 = 11	22 - 7 = 15	27 - 17 = 10
24 - 10 = 14	18 - 9 = 9	22 - 9 = 13	27 - 11 = 16
14 - 3 = 11	28 - 9 = 19	21 - 9 = 12	27 - 12 = 15
24 - 13 = 11	28 - 19 = 9	21 - 5 = 16	27 - 13 = 14
4 + 10 = 14	27 - 8 = 19	21 - 8 = 13	27 - 15 = 12
23 - 10 = 13	26 - 9 = 17	21 - 6 = 15	27 - 16 = 11
13 - 4 = 9	26 - 24 = 2	25 - 15 = 10	25 - 24 = 1
23 - 14 = 9	24 - 22 = 2	26 - 8 = 18	25 - 20 = 5
10 + 6 = 16	24 - 4 = 20	26 - 18 = 8	24 - 13 = 11
21 - 10 = 11	25 - 5 = 20	24 - 8 = 16	26 - 15 = 11
11 - 6 = 5	8 - 5 = 3	24 - 6 = 18	25 - 12 = 13

Exercise II

What number and 10 make 20?	*Ans:* 10
What number and 9 make 18?	*Ans:* 9
What number and 12 make 26?	*Ans:* 14
What number and 8 make 24?	*Ans:* 16
What number and 17 make 27?	*Ans:* 10
What number and 17 make 28?	*Ans:* 11
What number and 12 make 22?	*Ans:* 10
What number and 12 make 24?	*Ans:* 12
What number and 15 make 26?	*Ans:* 11
What number and 13 make 25?	*Ans:* 12
What number and 21 make 28?	*Ans:* 7
What number and 5 make 24?	*Ans:* 19
What number and 1 make 29?	*Ans:* 28
What number and 11 make 22?	*Ans:* 11
What number and 11 make 23?	*Ans:* 12
What number and 14 make 25?	*Ans:* 11
What number and 14 make 28?	*Ans:* 14
What number and 19 make 24?	*Ans:* 5
What number and 17 make 23?	*Ans:* 6
What number and 7 make 24?	*Ans:* 17

Exercise III

30 - 2 = 28	30 - 27 = 3	30 - 12 = 18	30 - 15 = 15
30 - 12 = 18	30 - 8 = 22	30 - 20 = 10	30 - 16 = 14
30 - 22 = 8	30 - 18 = 12	30 - 21 = 9	30 - 24 = 6
30 - 7 = 23	30 - 10 = 20	30 - 29 = 1	30 - 14 = 16
30 - 17 = 13	30 - 11 = 19	30 - 25 = 5	30 - 4 = 26

Word Problems

1. Blair replaced 20 light bulbs out of 30. How many more need to be replaced? *Ans:* 10 light bulbs.

2. The North Bridge is 28 feet long and the South Bridge is 10 feet shorter than that. How long is the South Bridge? *Ans:* 18 feet.

3. La is 28 years old.
    a) Le is 7 years younger than La. How old is Le? *Ans:* 21 years old.
    b) Li is 10 years younger than La. How old is Li? *Ans:* 18 years old.
    c) Lo is 11 years younger than La. How old is Lo? *Ans:* 17 years old.

    Solution: we can break 11 into 10 and 1. Then, 28 - 10 is 18, and 18 - 1 = 17.
    d) Lu is 18 years younger than La. How old is Lu? *Ans:* 10 years old.

4. A cab driver had 15 passengers yesterday and 26 today. How many more passengers did he have today than yesterday? *Ans:* 11 passengers.

5. There were 27 children on a school bus.
    a) At the first stop, 8 children got off. How many stayed on the bus? *Ans:* 19 children.
    b) At the second stop, 12 more children got off. How many stayed? *Ans:* 7 children.

6. Mom asked Fatima to share 22 raspberries with her twin brother, Jamal. Fatima took 12. Was she fair? *Ans:* Not really.

    Solution: It is not fair, because 22 - 12 = 10. Fatima left less berries for her brother than she took herself. Fair would have been 11.

7. The children counted 28 urchins and 14 starfish. How many more urchins than starfish did they find? *Ans:* 14 more urchins than starfish.

8. Trisha is 21. For her birthday, she received 19 presents. How many more does she need to have exactly 21 presents? *Ans:* 2 presents (21 - 19 = 2).

9. It takes 30 minutes to bake a chicken and only 23 minutes have passed. How many minutes are left until the chicken is ready? *Ans:* 7 minutes.

10. There are 28 days in February.
    a) After 9 days, how many days are left until the end of the month? *Ans:* 19 days.
    b) After 11 days? *Ans:* 17 days.
    c) After 14 days? *Ans:* 14 days.
    d) After 17 days? *Ans:* 11 days.

11. Out of 27 birds on the lake, 11 are swans and the rest are ducks. How many ducks are on the lake? *Ans:* 16 ducks.

12. Uncle Val tried to blow out 25 candles on his birthday cake but got only 18 on his first try. How many are still burning? *Ans:* 7 candles.

13. A mover placed 13 suitcases on one truck and 15 on the other. How many suitcases were there? *Ans:* 28 suitcases.

14. My 14 rabbits ate 26 carrots. Ed's 15 rabbits ate only 19. How many rabbits do we have together? *Ans:* 29 rabbits.
    a) How many more carrots did my rabbits eat? *Ans:* 7 carrots.

15. A 30-foot rope was cut into two pieces, and one piece was 15 feet. How long was the other piece? *Ans:* 15 feet.

16. Grandfather was cleaning his clock and laid 27 parts on the table. Jack decided to put them back together, but when he finished, 8 parts remained. How many parts did he put back together?
    Ans: 19 parts. Do you think Jack will be in trouble when the grandpa comes home from his walk?

17. Out of 29 students, 14 voted for Kirsten for class president and everyone else voted for Latisha. How many voted for Latisha?
    Ans: 15 students. Who won? Latisha, of course; she got more votes.

18. Lazlo found an old 30-piece jigsaw puzzle, but there were only 23 pieces in the box. How many were missing? *Ans:* 7 pieces.

19. Valerie's grandma knows 29 bedtime stories. She told Valerie 18 stories. How many stories has Valerie not heard yet? *Ans:* 11 stories.

20. Mom bought 30 birthday candles but used only 12 so far. How many unused candles are there? *Ans:* 18 candles.

21. A farmer had 30 sheep and sold 18 of them. How many did he keep? *Ans:* 12 sheep.

22. Harry and I carved 23 pumpkins altogether. I carved 14. How many did Harry carve? *Ans:* 9 pumpkins.

23. Sam learned 23 new spelling words and quickly forgot 8. How many does she still remember? *Ans:* 15 words.

24. Kerry's hens laid 27 eggs in two weeks. During the first week, they laid 14. How many did they lay in the second week? *Ans:* 13 eggs.

25. Two counties have 27 libraries altogether. If one county has 12, how many libraries are in the other county? *Ans:* 15 libraries.

26. There were 29 moths, but only 14 flew toward the lamp. How many didn't? *Ans:* 15 moths.

27. A dog and the leash cost $26 altogether. The leash cost $7. How much did the dog cost? *Ans:* $19.

28. Two snakes head to tail are 22 feet long. One snake is 14 feet. How long is the other? *Ans:* 8 feet.

29. Bill and Bob together have 30 pigs. If Bill has 19, how many does Bob have? *Ans:* 11 pigs.

30. There are 23 apartments in a building and 19 of them are rented. How many are empty? *Ans:* 4 apartments.

31. There are 23 pirates on the ship.
    a) 15 have beards. How many don't?
       Ans: 8 pirates.
    b) 9 have swords and the rest - pistols. How many have pistols?
       Ans: 14 pirates.
    c) 11 wear red pants and the rest wear blue ones. How many wear blue?
       Ans: 12 pirates.

32. A musician played 26 notes. Eight were out of tune. How many were good? *Ans:* 18 notes.

33. Twenty-seven Cub Scouts saw a banana slug and 11 of them cried. How many didn't? *Ans:* 16 scouts.

34. Twenty-five Girl Scouts saw a bat and 12 screamed. How many didn't? *Ans:* 13 scouts.

35. A magician showed 24 cards and then there were only 8. How many disappeared? *Ans:* 16 cards.

36. A student wrote 21 words on a board and then erased 14. How many did he leave on the board? *Ans:* 7 words.

37. Out of 24 birds on the wire, 19 just flew in. How many were already there? *Ans:* 5 birds.

38. A squirrel found some nuts. 13 nuts were rotten but 16 nuts were good. How many nuts did it find in total? *Ans:* 29 nuts (both good and bad).

39. Matt threw darts 26 times. He hit the target 17 times. How many times did he miss? *Ans:* 9 times.

40. A sumo wrestler had 25 matches. If he won 18, how many did he lose? *Ans:* 7 matches.

41. A cowboy threw his lasso 30 times and got it right 19 times. How many times did he get it wrong? *Ans:* 11 times.

42. A birdwatcher listened to 24 bird songs and guessed 19 of them correctly. How many songs did he not guess correctly? *Ans:* 5 songs.

43. Out of 26 light bulbs, 7 burned out in one month. How many didn't? *Ans:* 19 light bulbs.

44. Carla and June paid $27 for the soccer ball. June paid $19. How much did Carla pay? *Ans:* $8.

45. A janitor bought 22 brushes and used 19. How many new brushes does he still have? *Ans:* 3 brushes.

46. The tape was 30 yards. Milo used 18 yards. How much of the tape is left? *Ans:* 12 yards.

47. A lizard is 24 inches long. Its tail is 8 inches long. How long is the rest of his body? *Ans:* 16 inches.

48. A child has 21 teeth. Only 7 are permanent teeth and the rest are baby teeth. How many baby teeth does she have? *Ans:* 14 teeth.

49. A hungry giant saw 26 melons on a patch. He gobbled 19. How many did he leave untouched? *Ans:* 7 melons.

50. Two books cost $25. One book cost $17. How much is the other? *Ans:* $8.

51. Twenty-nine tribes lived in the valley but 16 tribes moved out. How many stayed? *Ans:* 13 tribes.

Adding and subtracting numbers up to 30

How many double-digit number pairs make 30?
Ans: 6 : 10 and 20; 11 and 19; 12 and 18; 13 and 17; 14 and 16; 15 and 15

Exercise I

1. The difference between two numbers is 10. If one number is 12, what's the other? *Ans:* 2 or 22
2. The difference between two numbers is 7. If one number is 15, what's the other? *Ans:* 22 or 8
3. The difference between two numbers is 18. If one number is 12, what's the other? *Ans:* 30 or 6
4. The difference between two numbers is 9. If one number is 13, what's the other? *Ans:* 22 or 4
5. The difference between two numbers is 16. If one number is 9, what's the other? *Ans:* 25 or 7
6. The difference between two numbers is 21. If one number is 5, what's the other? *Ans:* 26 or 16
7. The difference between two numbers is 13. If one number is 15, what's the other? *Ans:* 28 or 2
8. The difference between two numbers is 27. If one number is 14, what's the other? *Ans:* 13 or 13
9. The difference between two numbers is 12. If one number is 19, what's the other? *Ans:* 31 or 7
10. The difference between two numbers is 14. If one number is 14, what's the other? *Ans:* 28 or 0

Exercise II

12 - 7 = 5	15 + 7 - 2 = 10	17 + 8 - 3 = 22	31 - 10 = 20
6 + 5 - 3 = 8	18 + 7 - 11 = 14	19 - 5 + 6 = 20	32 - 11 = 21
12 + 4 - 7 = 9	16 - 3 + 7 = 20	12 + 11 = 23	31 - 20 = 11
14 - 3 + 4 = 15	16 - 8 + 4 = 12	12 + 13 = 25	32 - 12 = 20
17 - 9 + 4 = 10	17 + 8 - 10 = 15	12 + 15 = 27	32 - 13 = 19
16 + 5 - 8 = 3	16 + 7 - 3 = 20	12 + 14 = 26	32 - 16 = 16
4 + 7 - 2 = 9	13 + 8 - 5 = 24	30 - 10 = 20	32 - 14 = 18

Word Problems

1. Audrey wrote 19 spelling words and Jan wrote 7. How many words did they write together? *Ans:* 26 words.

2. Blake saved $14 and received $13 as a gift from his uncle. How much money does he have? *Ans:* $27.

3. There were 18 sailors on one boat and 9 on the other. How many sailors were on both boats? *Ans:* 27 sailors.

4. Gary has 25 teeth. If 12 teeth are on the bottom of his mouth, how many teeth are on the top? *Ans:* 13 teeth.

5. At the party, 16 out of 28 kids asked for soda. The rest wanted orange juice. How many children asked for OJ? *Ans:* 12 kids.

6. My uncle is 18. My aunt is 9 years older. How old is my aunt? *Ans:* 27 years.

7. Gaston is 19 years old.
    a) How old he will be in 7 years? *Ans:* 26 years old.
    b) In 9 years? *Ans:* 28 years old.
    c) In 10 years? *Ans:* 29 years old.
    d) In 11 years? *Ans:* 30 years old.

8. Manju has 17 apple seeds in her left hand and 7 in her right. How many seeds are in both her hands? *Ans:* 24 seeds.
    a) She planted 15 seeds. How many seeds did she keep? *Ans:* 9 seeds.

9. 3-year-old Lin turned the light on 12 times and off 11 times. How many times did he flip the switch? *Ans:* 23 times. Why is he doing this?

10. A rabbit weighs 8 pounds; a fox is 18 pounds. How much more does the fox weigh? *Ans:* 10 pounds.

11. I blew out 19 candles on mom's birthday cake, and my brother blew out another 9. How old is my mom? *Ans:* 28 years old.

12. Josh launched his toy helicopter 19 times and crashed it 11 times. How many times did he land it safely? *Ans:* 8 times.

13. A pair of shoes cost $21 and a pair of socks cost only $8. How much do they cost together? *Ans:* $29.

14. Barack had $13. He borrowed $11 and spent $8. How much is left? *Ans:* $16.

    Solution: $13 + $11 = $24. Out of $24, Lyle spent $8. $24 - $8 = $16.

15. At the garage sale, Hilary sold a parrot for $15 and a cage for $13. She then took all her money and bought a spotted guinea pig for $19. How much money was left?
Ans: $9 (15 + 13 = 28, 28 - 19 = 9).

16. Thirteen birds sat on a wire. Then, 11 more birds came, and 15 birds flew away. How many birds are now on the wire?
Ans: 9 (13 + 11 = 24, then 24 - 15 = 9).

17. A restaurant chef took a dozen (12) eggs from one basket and 6 eggs from the other. He only used 18 eggs. How many eggs are left?
Ans: 0 or none. Don't be tricked by the word "only."

18. Floyd had 25 dollars. He spent $14, and then earned $12. How much money does he have now? *Ans:* $23.

19. There were 19 DVDs in Paul's video library. He gave 7 to his friends and borrowed 12 DVDs from them. How many DVDs are in Paul's library now? *Ans:* 24 (19 - 7 = 12, 12 + 12 = 24).

20. Fran must collect 30 signatures. Yesterday, she collected 17; today, 9 more. How many signatures does she need? *Ans:* 4.

    Solution: 17 signatures yesterday + 9 today = 26.
    Then, 30 signatures needed - 26 collected = 4 more to go.

21. Granny Smith picked 30 apples from 3 trees. She picked 16 from the first and 6 from the second tree. How many apples did granny Smith pick from the third tree? *Ans:* 8 apples.

    Solution: 30 apples - 16 (from the first tree) = 14 (from the second and the third). Now, 14 - 6 (from the second tree) = 8 apples left that must have came from the third tree.

22. A truck's tank can hold 29 gallons of gasoline. At a gas station, we bought 18 gallons to fill up the tank. How many gallons of gas were in the tank before we got gasoline? *Ans:* 11 gallons.

    Solution: The whole tank is 29 gallons - 18 we put in to fill it up = 11 gallons were there before we filled up the tank.

23. There are 26 letters in our alphabet. There are 5 vowels, 2 semivowels, and the rest are consonants. How many consonants are there?
Ans: 19 consonants.

24. I paid $29 for 3 plants. The first plant cost $7; the second was also $7. How much did the third plant cost?
Ans: $15 (29 - 7 = 22, 22 - 7 = 15).

25. Mr. Envelope needs 29 cents worth of stamps for a letter. He has a 8-cent and a 15-cent stamp. What much more in stamps does he need to buy? *Ans:* 6 cents.

    Solution: 8-cent stamp + 15-cent stamp = 23 cents worth of stamps that Mr. Envelop has already. Now, 29 cents (needed for the letter) - 23 cents (he already has) = 6 cents more.

26. Mackenzie caught 4 bugs and counted 26 legs. The first bug had 6 legs, the second bug had 6 legs, and the third bug also had 6 legs. How many legs did the last bug have? *Ans:* 8 legs.

    Solution: Three bugs out of four that Mackenzie caught have 6 + 6 + 6 = 18 legs. Now, 26 legs (all four bugs) - 18 legs (already counted on three bugs) = 8 legs (the fourth bug). I think the last bug is a spider. Ah-ah-ah!

27. There are 26 pages in the town's newspaper. One page covers the news, 9 pages are sports, and 9 pages are arts & music. The rest are the ads. How many pages are the ads? *Ans:* 7 pages.

    Solutions: 26 pages -1 page (news) = 25 pages; 25 pages - 9 pages (sports) = 16 pages; 16 pages - 9 pages (art & music) = 7 pages left for the ads.
    Or we add all the pages, 1 + 9 + 9 = 19 pages of news, sports, and art & music. Then, 26 - 19 = 7 pages are left for the ads.

28. Brady laid out bricks in a triangle: 11 bricks on one side and 11 bricks on the other side. How many bricks did he use for the third side if altogether there were 30 bricks? *Ans:* 8 bricks.

    Solution: 30 - 11 (one side) = 29, then 29 - 11 (the other side) = 8 bricks.
    11 + 11 = 22 (bricks on two sides), then 30 - 22 = 8 bricks on the third side.

29. Fifteen birds were sitting on the wires.
    a) Then, 18 new birds came and 11 birds flew away. How many birds are there now? *Ans:* 22 birds (15 + 18 = 33, 33 - 11 = 22).
    b) Then, 17 more birds came and 28 flew away. How many birds are there now? *Ans:* 11 birds (12 + 17 = 39, 39 - 28 = 11).
    c) After that, another 11 birds came and sat on the wires. How many birds are there now? *Ans:* 22 birds.
    d) Now, 9 birds flew away and 2 new birds arrived. How many birds will we see now? *Ans:* 15 birds, but these are different birds.

30. At an archery competition, 24 arrows were fired. Of these arrows, 3 broke and 4 were lost. How many arrows were returned? *Ans:* 17 arrows.

31. The town planned 24 shows for a 3-day celebration. The first day, there were 8 shows; on the second day, there were also 8. How many shows were left for the third day? *Ans:* 8 shows.

32. On a 20-mile hike, our team ran 7 miles uphill, 7 miles downhill and we walked the rest of the trail. How many miles did we walk? *Ans:* 6 miles.

33. Professor Bookworm borrowed 14 books from the library. The next week, he returned 7 and borrowed another 14 books. How many books does the professor have now? *Ans:* 21 books.

34. There were 12 goldfish in a fishbowl. I took out 6 goldfish and put in 12 guppies. How many fish are in the fishbowl now?
    Ans: 18 fish.

35. We bought 3 tickets for the theater. Each ticket was $8.
    a) How much money did we spend? *Ans:* $24 (8 + 8 + 8 = 24).
    b) We had to return one ticket and got our money back. What is the price of 2 remaining tickets? *Ans:* $16 (24 - 8 = 16).

36. Jake put 25 books in his backpack. Then, he took 10 books out. Then he changed his mind and put 5 books back in the backpack. How many books are in the backpack? *Ans:* 20 books (25 - 10 + 5 = 20).

37. Eleven ducks and 14 swans lived in a pond. One day, 8 birds took off to the south. How many stayed back?
    Ans: 17 birds (11 + 14 = 25; then, 25 - 8 = 17).

38. A month has 22 working days and 8 weekend days. How many days are in this month? *Ans:* 30 days.

39. A month has 30 days. There were 9 weekend days and 1 holiday. How many working days are in the month? *Ans:* 20 days.

40. There are 14 birch trees and 14 oaks in the park. 19 trees have bird nests in them. How many trees don't have any nests? *Ans:* 9 trees.

41. During the basketball game, our team was 16 points ahead. Then, we lost 8 points. Then we scored 12 points, and at the end lost another 14 points. Did we win? *Ans:* Yes.
    a) How many points ahead of the other team were we at the end of the game? *Ans:* We were 6 points ahead (16 - 8 = 8; 8 + 12 = 20; 20 - 14 = 6).

42. Mario bought 12 sticks of orange bubble gum and 15 sticks of the banana flavor. He he hid 9 sticks in his pocket. How many sticks did he not hide?
    Ans: 18 (12 + 15 = 27; 27 - 9 = 18).

43. There were 14 strawberries and 14 gooseberries. I dipped 19 berries in chocolate. How many berries didn't I dip?
    Ans: 9 berries (14 + 14 = 28; 28 - 19 = 9).

44. Thirteen blue knights challenged 19 green knights to a jousting tournament, but only 7 knights showed up. How many stayed in their castles?
Ans: 12 knights. Not because they were afraid, but may be they had too much homework.

45. A library received 8 new novels, 13 mysteries and 2 comic books. Of these, it lent 7 books out right away. How many went on the shelves?
Ans: 16 books.

46. Twenty-five minutes were left before the show. It takes me 5 minutes to get ready, 12 minutes to drive and 6 minutes to buy tickets for the show. Will I get there on time?
Ans: Yes, because 5 + 12 + 6 = 23 minutes. But I better hurry!

47. A bird caught 17 flies and 13 mosquitoes. She gave 24 bugs to her babies. How many she kept for herself? *Ans:* 6 bugs.

48. Sixteen hikers and 14 bikers came for an overnight stay. There were only 19 beds in a local hotel. How many hikers and bikers slept outside?
Ans: 11.

49. A poet bought 12 roses and 18 lilies. He gave 15 flowers to one girl. How many did he give to the other? *Ans:* 15 flowers.

50. We had 11 large band-aids and 19 small ones at home. After Jorgen fell on a cactus we used 29 band-aids. How many are left for the next accident?
Ans: 1 band-aid.

Adding numbers up to 40

Exercise I

Count forward from 0 to 50 by 5 (i.e., 5, 10, 15, 20)
Count backward from 50 to 0 by 5 (i.e., 50, 45, 40, 35, etc.)

Exercise II

15 + 10 = 25	15 + 15 = 30	5 + 35 = 40	45 - 25 = 20
15 + 20 = 35	20 + 15 = 35	15 + 25 = 40	50 - 20 = 30
25 + 10 = 35	25 + 15 = 40	40 - 10 = 30	50 - 30 = 20
25 + 20 = 45	15 + 25 = 40	40 - 15 = 25	50 - 40 = 10
10 + 15 = 25	35 + 10 = 45	45 - 15 = 30	50 - 45 = 5
25 + 25 = 50	40 + 10 = 50	35 - 25 = 10	50 - 35 = 15
20 + 15 = 35	35 + 15 = 50	45 - 20 = 25	50 - 25 = 25

A trick reminder:

Remember to use this trick when adding numbers that end with 9. You can for the moment add 1 and then take 1 away at the end.

Problem: 17 + 19 =?

Solution: Step 1: Let's add 1 to 19; that's 20.
Step 2: Now, 17 + 20 = 37
Step 3: Now we have to take back 1, which we borrowed to make this problem easier.
37 - 1 = 36
Therefore, 17 + 19 = 36.

Exercise III

15 + 10 = 25	19 + 20 = 39	29 + 9 = 38	14 + 16 = 30
15 + 20 = 35	29 + 10 = 39	2 + 29 = 31	24 + 16 = 40
15 + 30 = 45	29 + 20 = 49	7 + 26 = 33	16 + 19 = 35
11 + 10 = 21	39 + 10 = 49	9 + 23 = 32	17 + 15 = 32
11 + 20 = 31	25 + 20 = 45	8 + 29 = 37	15 + 15 = 30
11 + 30 = 41	25 + 10 = 35	5 + 29 = 34	13 + 18 = 31
21 + 10 = 31	27 + 20 = 47	29 + 10 = 39	18 + 15 = 33
21 + 20 = 41	18 + 30 = 48	29 + 11 = 40	16 + 16 = 32
20 + 20 = 40	28 + 4 = 32	18 + 11 = 29	17 + 17 = 34
20 + 21 = 41	28 + 5 = 33	18 + 21 = 39	18 + 18 + 36
34 + 10 = 44	27 + 7 = 34	25 + 12 = 37	19 + 19 = 38
19 + 10 = 29	28 + 9 = 37	14 + 21 = 35	20 + 20 = 40

Word Problems

1. A policeman gave tickets to 20 jaywalkers and 5 litterbugs. How many tickets did he write in total? *Ans:* 25 tickets.

2. Nicole put 15 pillow cases and 10 hand towels in the washer. How many items did she put in the washer in total? *Ans:* 25 items.

3. It took 29 sections to build a fence. It took 4 sections to build a gate. How many sections did it take to build both? *Ans:* 33 sections.

4. For the concert, the teacher bought 20 tickets for the first row and 15 tickets for the second row. How many tickets did the teacher buy?
    Ans: 35 tickets.

5. A fisherman caught 20 more fish than the other. The other fisherman had only caught 10 fish. How many fish did they both catch? *Ans:* 40 fish.
    Solution: One fisherman caught 10 fish. The other caught 10 + 20 = 30 fish. Together, they caught 10 + 30 = 40 fish.

6. A teacher made 15 copies, then 10 more copies. How many copies did she make? *Ans:* 25 copies.

7. A squirrel weighs 5 pounds and a raccoon weighs 20 pounds more. How much do they weigh together? *Ans:* 30 pounds.
    Solution: Raccoon weighs 5 pounds + 20 pounds = 25 pounds. Both weigh 5 lb + 25 lb = 30 (pounds).

8. The volunteers made 25 cheese and 25 turkey sandwiches. Hungry Girl Scouts ate 45 sandwiches. How many were left for the volunteers?
    Ans: 5 sandwiches.

9. At the camp, we had 5 counselors and 25 campers. How many people were at the camp? *Ans:* 30 people.

10. Amber and Jade had $30. Amber spent $15 and Jade spent $10. How much money is left? *Ans:* $5.

11. A bicyclist, while going on a 40-mile trip, stops after 25 miles. How many miles does he still have to go? *Ans:* 15 miles.

12. A fisherman caught 35 fish and let 20 go. How many did he keep?
    Ans: 15 fish.

13. Nelly picked 15 apples and 25 pears, but on her way back she ate 20 fruits. How many fruits did she bring home?
    Ans: 20 fruits. She also had a stomach ache all day.

14. On the way to the park, Jasmine counted 5 red cars, 10 black cars and 15 beige ones. How many cars did she count? *Ans:* 30 cars.

15. How much is 5 plus 5, plus 5? *Ans:* 15.

16. How much is 5 plus 5, plus 5, plus 5? *Ans:* 20.

17. How much is 10 plus 10, plus 10? *Ans:* 30.

18. Take 15 add 10. Add another 10 and take away 25. How much is left? *Ans:* 10.

19. Take 40 and take away 15, add 25, take away 20. How much did you get? *Ans:* 30.

20. Take 30 and take away 25, take away 5, add 35. How much is it now? *Ans:* 35.

21. The game cost $30. I have $15, Cameron has $5, and Alex has $10. Do we have enough money to buy the game? *Ans:* Yes.

22. Getting ready for a test, Marissa put 5 pencils, 5 crayons, 5 pens, 5 erasers and 5 notebooks in her bag. How many items altogether did she take? *Ans:* 25 items.

23. There are 15 apples in one box and 10 in the other. I took 5 apples from the first box and 5 from the other. How many apples are now in both boxes together? *Ans:* 15 apples.

24. Natasha had to do 10 problems from the first book, 10 from the second and 10 from the third. She did 5 problems from each book. How many problems are left to do? *Ans:* 15 problems.

    Solution: Problems from all 3 books are 10 + 10 + 10 = 30 problems. Then 30 (problems from all three books) - 5 (problems from the 1st book) - 5 (problems from the 2nd book) - 5 (problems from the 3rd book) = 15 problems left in all 3 books.

25. We have 30 children in the choir. There 25 girls. How many boys are in the choir? *Ans:* 5 boys.

26. Out of 50 people in a construction crew, 25 are carpenters, 15 are roofers, 10 are plumbers and the rest are painters. How many painters are there? *Ans:* 0, there are no painters.

27. For the Dress-as-a-Pirate Party, 15 kids had patches on their left eyes, 20 on their right and the 10 had no eye patches at all. How many kids came? *Ans:* 45 kids (15 + 20 + 10).

28. A turtle laid 40 eggs, but only 20 eggs hatched. How many didn't? *Ans:* 20 eggs.

29. One hen laid 25 eggs and another laid 12. How many little chicks will hatch? *Ans:* 37 chicks.

30. A store sold 24 calendars before New Years Day and 14 calendars after. How many calendars did it sell? *Ans:* 38 calendars.

31. It took Bluebeard 17 minutes to shave the right side of his face and 16 minutes for the left side. How long did it take him for both sides? *Ans:* 33 minutes.

32. It took a princess 14 minutes to do one braid and 16 minutes for the other. How long did it take her to do two braids? *Ans:* 30 minutes.

33. The air pressure in a tire was 24 units. Clive put in 15 more units. How many units of pressure are in the tire now? *Ans:* 39 units.

34. A roofer took 18 tiles from one stack and 13 from the other. How many tiles did he take? *Ans:* 31 tiles.

35. Tony caught 25 mice and 9 rats in the barn. How many pests did Tony catch? *Ans:* 34 pests. Tony is a dog who thinks he is a cat.

36. A gardener pruned 19 rose bushes at one house and 15 at the other. How many rose bushes did she prune? *Ans:* 34 bushes.

37. A hotel maid made 14 beds on the first floor and 19 beds on the second floor. How many beds did she make? *Ans:* 33 beds.

38. Because of bad weather, the passengers had to wait 24 hours and then 7 more hours for their airplane. How long was the wait? *Ans:* 31 hours.

39. Two teams practiced in the Olympic pool. The first team had 17 swimmers and the other had 18. How many swimmers practiced that day? *Ans:* 35 swimmers.

40. One day in the fall, Rona counted 18 leaves that had fallen from the birch tree. The next day, 15 more leaves fell. How many leaves fell from the tree? *Ans:* 33 leaves.

41. Jenny bought two cartons of milk with 16 ounces in each carton. How many ounces of milk did she buy? *Ans:* 32 ounces.

42. Vince and Vance went fishing. Each of them caught 17 fish. How many fish did both catch? *Ans:* 34 fish.

43. Two pieces of 18-foot rope were tied together. How long is the new rope? *Ans:* 36 feet. May be less.

44. Sandy made a new necklace out of two old ones. The old necklaces had 20 beads each. How many beads are in the new necklace? *Ans:* 40 beads.

45. An office has one room with 18 desks and the other with 19 desks. How many desks are in both rooms? *Ans:* 37 desks.

46. Miriam had $19 in her pocket and $15 in her wallet. How much money is in both? *Ans:* $34.

47. A gallery had 16 china vases and 18 glass vases. How many vases are there? *Ans:* 34 vases.

48. A diver scared away 27 stingrays and 9 sharks. How many fish did she scare away? *Ans:* 36 fish.

49. A healer made a potion with 12 exotic herbs and 19 roots. How many herbs and roots did he use? *Ans:* 31 herbs and roots.

50. Tom has 13 transformers. Tim has 5 more transformers than Tom. How many transformers do both have? *Ans:* 31 transformers.
Solution: 13 + 5 = 18 (transformers that Tim has).
Now, 13 (Tom's) + 18 (Tim's) = 31(both).

51. In a small school, the first grade has 21 students. The second grade has 2 students fewer. How many students are in both grades? *Ans:* 40 students.
Solution: 21 - 2 = 19 (students in the second class).
Then, 21 (first grade) + 19 (second grade) = 40 (students in both grades).

52. One gallery has 17 pictures; the other gallery has 5 more. How many pictures are in both galleries? *Ans:* 39 pictures (17 + 5 = 22, 17 + 22 = 39).

Subtracting two-digit numbers

Trick

Taking a two-digit number from another two-digit number can be helped with a little trick. All you need to do is to take the second number and break it into 2 parts. For example, if you need to solve 40 - 17 = ?, break 17 into 10 and 7. Then, 40 - 10 = 30, and 30 - 7 = 23.

Problem: 37 - 23 = ?
Solution: Step 1: We can say that 23 equals 20 + 3.
Step 2: Then 37 - 23 would be 37 - 20, which is 17, then take away 3.
37 - 20 = 17, 17 - 3 = 14.
The answer: 37 - 23 = 14.

Problem: 35 - 27 = ?
Solution: Step 1: We can say that 27 equals 20 + 7.
Step 2: Then 35 - 27 would be 35 - 20 and then take away 7.
35 - 20 = 15, 15 - 7 = 8.
The answer: 35 - 27 = 8.

Exercise I

Count backwards from 40 by 2.
Count backwards from 40 by 3.
Count backwards from 40 by 4.
Count backwards from 50 by 5.

Exercise II

35 - 6 = 29	33 - 25 = 8	33 - 15 = 18	35 - 19 = 16
35 - 16 = 19	36 - 9 = 27	39 - 3 = 36	35 - 29 = 6
29 - 7 = 22	36 - 19 = 17	39 - 13 = 26	33 - 4 = 29
29 - 17 = 12	25 - 7 = 18	39 - 23 = 16	33 - 14 = 19
33 - 5 = 28	25 - 17 = 8	39 - 33 = 6	33 - 24 = 9
33 - 15 = 18	33 - 5 = 28	35 - 9 = 26	38 - 14 = 24

Exercise III

40 - 2 = 38	40 - 18 = 22	40 - 27 = 13	40 - 35 = 5
40 - 12 = 28	40 - 28 = 12	40 - 37 = 3	40 - 6 = 34
40 - 22 = 18	40 - 38 = 2	40 - 5 = 35	40 - 16 = 24
40 - 32 = 8	40 - 7 = 33	40 - 15 = 25	40 - 26 = 24
40 - 8 = 32	40 - 17 = 23	40 - 25 = 15	40 - 36 = 4

Word Problems

1. Erin had 34 dolls and gave away 13. How many does she have now?
    Ans: 21 dolls.

2. This month, we had 19 rainy days and 9 days without rain. How many days were in this month? *Ans:* 28 days.
    a) What month was it?
       Ans: February. February has 28 days, other months have more days.

3. Kris invited 32 people and only 27 came. How many couldn't come?
    Ans: 5 people.

4. There are 38 skiers in the emergency room. Fifteen have casts on their legs, and the rest have casts on their arms. How many have casts on their arms? *Ans:* 23 skiers.

5. There were 24 inches of snow but overnight 8 more inches of snow fell on the ground. How many inches of snow are there now?
    Ans: 32 inches.

6. The school bus has 38 passenger seats.
    a) If there are 14 on board, how many more students can get on the bus?
       Ans: 24 students.
    b) If there are 11, how many more can get on this bus? *Ans:* 27 students.
    c) If there are 25, how many more can get on this bus? *Ans:* 13 students.
    d) If there are 19, how many more can get on this bus? *Ans:* 19 students.

7. Out of 33 test words, Owen made mistakes on 15. How many words did he spell correctly? *Ans:* 18 words.

8. There were 33 children in Mr. Curly's class.
    a) If there were 22 girls, how many boys were in the class? *Ans:* 11 boys.
    b) If there were 19 girls, how many boys were in the class? *Ans:* 14 boys.
    c) If there were 17 girls, how many boys were in the class? *Ans:* 16 boys.
    d) If there were 15 girls, how many boys were in the class? *Ans:* 18 boys.

9. There were 34 tarantulas in a jar in a lab and then there were 18. How many escaped? *Ans:* 16 tarantulas. I won't be visiting this lab.

10. A mad scientist wrote 33 secret formulas and then crossed out 15. How many did he keep? *Ans:* 18 formulas.

11. If 26 out of 31 watermelons have seeds, how many don't?
    Ans: 5 watermelons.

12. After a farmer sold 14 pumpkins out of 40, how many are left?
    Ans: 26 pumpkins.

13. Thirty-nine tourists came to the zoo and 28 left by noon. How many are still in the zoo? *Ans:* 11 tourists.

14. Tory tossed a basketball 40 times and missed 17. How many times did she score? *Ans:* 23 times.

15. Out of 40 coins in a pirate's treasure chest, 26 were gold and the rest were silver. How many silver coins were in the chest? *Ans:* 14 coins.

16. If you have $40 and pay $14 for a necklace and $18 for a pair of earrings, how much money will you have left over? *Ans:* $8.

    Solution:
    One way: $40 -$14 (for the necklace) = $26, $26 - $18 (for the earrings) = $8
    Another way: $14 (necklace) + $18 (earrings) = $32 (for both), $40 - $32 = $8

17. When the smaller of two numbers is 28 and the difference is 7, what is the larger number? *Ans:* 35.

18. When the larger of two numbers is 37 and the difference is 15, what is the smaller number? *Ans:* 22.

19. When the smaller of two numbers is 23 and the difference is 17, what is the larger number? *Ans:* 40.

20. When the smaller of two numbers is 27 and the difference is 9, what is the larger number? *Ans:* 36.

21. When the larger of two numbers is 35 and the difference is 11, what is the smaller number? *Ans:* 24.

22. Len and Mustafa caught 37 little garden snakes together. If Mustafa caught 19, how many did Len catch? *Ans:* 18 snakes.

23. Which one is bigger, 14 + 17 or 19 + 13?
    Ans: The second sum, because 14 + 17 = 31 and 19 + 13 = 32.

24. On a golf course, 36 golfers stumbled upon 29 gophers. How many more golfers were there than gophers? *Ans:* 7 more golfers than gophers.

25. A carousel has 17 seats and 35 children are waiting in line. How many kids will have to take the second ride? *Ans:* 18 children.

26. In the closet, there were 26 empty boxes and 11 boxes filled with clothes. How many boxes were in the closet? *Ans:* 37 boxes.

27. There were 40 children on a school bus. At a stop, 16 children got out. How many stayed on the bus? *Ans:* 24 children.

28. In one day, Bill told 40 lies and 27 truths. How many more lies than truths did Bill tell? *Ans:* 13 more lies.

29. When a fisherman stepped in the water, he was surrounded by 40 hungry piranhas. He chased 39 piranhas away. How many fish did he not scare? *Ans:* 1 fish.

30. Tanisha has 40 braids. 27 have green ribbons and the rest have yellow ribbons. How many yellow ribbons does she have?
    Ans: 13 yellow ribbons.

31. Ali-Baba was chased by 40 thieves.
    a) If 27 thieves wore turbans, how many didn't? *Ans:* 13 thieves.
    b) If 18 thieves had an earring, how many didn't? *Ans:* 22 thieves.
    c) If 24 thieves wore shoes, how many didn't? *Ans:* 14 thieves.
    d) If 15 thieves had scars, how many didn't? *Ans:* 25 thieves.

32. If out of 32 teeth, an old person lost 15 of his teeth. How many are still left? *Ans:* 17 teeth.

33. I put 36 paper sheets in a printer and made 18 copies. How many sheets are left in the printer? *Ans:* 18 sheets.

34. A store received 28 television sets and sold 14. How many were not sold? *Ans:* 14 sets.

35. A chef had 32 eggs and used 16 for breakfast. How many eggs were left in the fridge? *Ans:* 16 eggs.

36. There were 38 dancers on the stage and 18 of them were girls. How many boys danced? *Ans:* 20 boys.

37. Out of 26 pieces of firewood, 13 were burned. How many pieces were left? *Ans:* 13 pieces.

38. Out of 36 sterile surgical gloves, Doctor Cutter used 18. How many were not used? *Ans:* 18 gloves.

39. Out of 35 toys in a box, 16 are broken. How many are good?
    Ans: 19 toys.

40. Out of 37 text messages Vivian received, she only replied to 19 of them. How many messages were ignored? *Ans:* 18 messages.

41. A chef cooked 40 snails, but the guests ate only 20. How many were left on the plates? *Ans:* 20 snails.

42. The chef put 40 crab cakes on 2 plates. He put 19 cakes on the first plate. How many cakes went on the other plate? *Ans:* 21 crab cakes.

43. The chef used 40 cherry tomatoes for 2 salads. If there were 22 tomatoes in the first salad, how many were in the other? *Ans:* 18 tomatoes.

44. After dinner, the bus boy picked up 40 forks and knives. If there were 23 forks, how many knives did he pick up? *Ans:* 17 knives.

45. Out of 40 gallons of gas in the tank, 25 were used during the trip. How many gallons are still in the tank? *Ans:* 15 gallons.

46. In a cherry orchard, out of 39 trees, 23 are already blooming. How many more will bloom soon? *Ans:* 16 trees.

47. Eric hung 35 pieces of clothing on the line. Two hours later, he found only 23 pieces. How many pieces of clothing did he lose? *Ans:* 12 pieces.

48. An oracle (an ancient person who could tell the future) made 33 predictions, but only 11 predictions came true. How many didn't?
Ans: 22 predictions.

49. A writer wrote 33 pages in one day but then tore 24 pages in frustration. How many pages of writing did he keep?
Ans: 9 pages. Writing can be very hard sometimes.

50. After Valerie took 7 cookies from the cookie sheet, there were still 29 cookies left. How many cookies were on the sheet at first?
Ans: 36 cookies (29 + 7 = 36).

51. On a 40 minutes walk, my dog got tired and I had to carry him for the last 19 minutes. How many minutes did my dog walk by himself?
Ans: 21 minutes.

Doubling, tripling, and quadrupling up to 50

Doubling, as you remember, is to add two equal numbers together. Tripling means adding together three equal numbers, and quadrupling will be adding 4 numbers together. Later on we will learn how to multiply, a clever shortcut for adding number quickly and accurately. But for now, we will learn to add.

Problem: 17 + 17 = ?
There are two ways to approach this problem:

First Solution: Step 1: The number 17 is made of 10 and 7.
                      Step 2: Then 17 + 17 can be solved 17 + 10 = 27, and then 27 + 7 = 34
                      Therefore: 17 + 17 = 34.

Second Solution: Step 1: The numbers 17 are made of 10 and 7.
                      Step 2: Then 17 + 17 can be solved by separately adding tens and ones, so 10 + 10 = 20 and 7 + 7 = 14.
                      Step 3: Then 20 + 14 = 34
                      Therefore: 17 + 17 = 34.

Problem: 13 + 13 + 13 = ?
First Solution: 13 + 13 = 26, then 26 + 13 = 39
Second Solution: 13 = 10 + 3. We will add tens 10 + 10 + 10 = 30, then we add ones 3 + 3 + 3 = 9.
                      Therefore: 30 + 9 = 39.

Exercise I

10 + 10 = 20	13 + 13 + 13 = 39	10 + 10 + 10 + 10 = 40
10 + 10 + 10 = 30	14 + 14 = 28	10 + 10 + 10 + 10 + 10 = 50
20 + 10 = 30	14 + 14 + 14 = 42	11 + 11 + 11 + 11 = 44
20 + 20 = 40	15 + 15 = 30	20 + 20 = 40
11 + 11 = 22	15 + 15 + 15 = 45	21 + 21 = 42
11 + 11 + 11 = 33	16 + 16 = 32	22 + 22 = 44
22 + 11 = 33	16 + 16 + 16 = 48	23 + 23 = 46
12 + 12 = 24	17 + 17 = 34	24 + 24 = 48
12 + 12 + 12 = 36	18 + 18 = 36	25 + 25 = 50
13 + 13 = 26	19 + 19 = 38	20 + 20 + 10 = 50

Word Problems

1. Jared has 10 coins in one hand and 10 in the other. How many coins is he holding? *Ans:* 20 coins.

2. Sophia spent 7 days with one grandparent and 7 days with the other. How many days did she spend with both grandparents? *Ans:* 14 days.

3. One octopus has 8 legs.
    a) How many legs do two octopi have? *Ans:* 16 legs.
    b) How many legs do three octopi have? *Ans:* 24 legs.
    c) How many legs do four octopi have? *Ans:* 32 legs.

4. One guitar has 6 strings.
    a) How many strings are on 2 guitars? *Ans:* 12 strings.
    b) How many strings are on 3 guitars? *Ans:* 18 strings.
    c) How many strings are on 4 guitars? *Ans:* 24 strings.

5. There are 11 photos in one album and 11 in the other. How many photos are in both? *Ans:* 22 photos.

6. A book shelf holds 7 books.
    a) How many books could fit on two shelves? *Ans:* 14 books.
    b) How many books could fit on three shelves? *Ans:* 21 books.
    c) How many books could fit on four shelves? *Ans:* 28 books.

7. One dozen is twelve.
    a) How much is two dozen? *Ans:* 24.
    b) How much is three dozen? *Ans:* 36.
    c) How much is four dozen? *Ans:* 48.

8. In a chess game, there are 16 white pieces and 16 black. How many pieces are on the chess board? *Ans:* 32 pieces.

9. There are 13 houses on the right side of the street and 13 houses on the other. How many houses are there? *Ans:* 26 houses.

10. There are 12 brown eggs in the basket and 12 white eggs. How many eggs are in the basket? *Ans:* 24 eggs.

11. A waiter put 17 spoons and 17 forks on the table. How many pieces of silverware did the waiter put on the table? *Ans:* 34 pieces.

12. A student turned in 14 pages of math work and 14 pages of English homework. How many pages did he turn in? *Ans:* 28 pages.

13. Marisa skipped 13 times on one foot and 13 times on the other. How many times did she skip? *Ans:* 26 times.

14. A picture framer made 15 large and 15 small picture frames. How many frames did he make in all? *Ans:* 30 frames.

15. Petra ran 16 minutes to the store and 16 minutes back. How many minutes did she run? *Ans:* 32 minutes.

16. The school band recorded 15 songs on one CD and 15 songs on another. How many songs did they record? *Ans:* 30 songs.

17. One spider has 8 legs.
    a) How many legs do 2 spiders have? *Ans:* 16 legs.
    b) How many legs do 3 spiders have? *Ans:* 24 legs.
    c) How many legs do 4 spiders have? *Ans:* 32 legs.

18. If one box of candies has 11 pieces,
    a) How many pieces do two boxes have? *Ans:* 22 pieces.
    b) How many pieces do three boxes have? *Ans:* 33 pieces.

19. After a nasty skateboarding accident, Hunter found 13 bruises on his right side and 13 on the left. How many bruises did he get altogether? *Ans:* 26 bruises.

20. Terry put 17 apples and 17 pears into a bowl. How many fruits are there? *Ans:* 34 fruits.

21. Glenn picked 13 raisins from a muffin and 13 raisins from a pudding. How many raisins did he pick? *Ans:* 26 raisins. Why did he do that?

22. If there are 18 spokes in one bicycle wheel, how many are in two wheels? *Ans:* 36 spokes.

23. If one person can milk 8 cows,a) How many cows can 2 people milk? *Ans:* 16 cows.
    b) How many cows can 3 people milk? *Ans:* 24 cows.
    c) How many cows can 4 people milk? *Ans:* 32 cows.

24. If one donkey can carry 9 sacks of hay,
    a) How many sacks can two donkeys carry? *Ans:* 18 sacks.
    b) How many sacks can three donkeys carry? *Ans:* 27 sacks.
    c) How many sacks can four donkeys carry? *Ans:* 36 sacks.

25. One battery can last 17 hours. How many hours can two batteries last? *Ans:* 34 hours.

26. If one steak costs $13,
    a) How much will two steaks cost? *Ans:* $26.
    b) How much will three steaks cost? *Ans:* $39.

27. There are 12 nuts in one pound of chestnuts.
    a) How many chestnuts are in two pounds? *Ans:* 24 nuts.
    b) How many chestnuts are in three pounds? *Ans:* 36 nuts.

28. Snow White had 7 apples.
    a) How many apples would 2 Snow Whites have? *Ans:* 14 apples.
    b) How many apples would 3 Snow Whites have? *Ans:* 21 apples.
    c) How many apples would 4 Snow Whites have? *Ans:* 28 apples.
    d) What if there were 5 Snow Whites? *Ans:* 35 apples.

29. Think about the Seven Dwarfs.
    a) How many right and left arms do 7 dwarfs have? *Ans:* 14 arms.
    b) How many right and left arms and right legs together do 7 dwarfs
       have? *Ans:* 21 of them.
    c) How many right and left arms and right and left legs do they have?
       Ans: 28 of them.

30. Boris paid $21 for a pet skunk. How much would he pay for two skunks?
    Ans: $42.

    Solution: Adding larger numbers is not that hard.
    Look, 21 is equal 20 + 1. First, we add tens, 20 + 20 = 40.
    Then we add ones, 1 + 1 = 2. Now 40 + 2 = 42 dollars for two pet skunk;
    but why would anyone have a skunk for a pet?

31. One ticket cost $23. How much do two tickets cost? *Ans:* $46.

32. One tree is 24 feet tall. How tall would a tree double this height be?
    Ans: 48 feet.

33. One melon has 25 seeds. How many seeds would be in two melons?
    Ans: 50 seeds.

34. One archer carries 14 arrows. How many arrows will three archers carry?
    Ans: 42 arrows.

    Solution: Adding three numbers is as easy as adding two. Let's sort it out.
    First let's add tens, 10 + 10 + 10 = 30. Now let's add ones; 4 + 4 + 4 = 12.
    Then, 30 + 12 = 42. Of course we can always add one number at a time:
    14 + 14 = 28. Then, 28 + 14 = 42.

35. If one cave has 15 bats, how many bats are in 3 caves? *Ans:* 45 bats.

36. If one piñata has 24 candies, how many candies are in two piñatas?
    Ans: 48 candies.

37. If it takes 19 days to paint one picture, how long will it take for two
    pictures? *Ans:* 38 days.

38. If one jump of a kangaroo is 18 feet, how long would two jumps be?
   Ans: 36 feet.

39. If Tally can buy 17 stickers for $1, how many can she buy for $2?
   Ans: 34 stickers.

40. If one soccer team has 11 players,
   a) How many players are in two teams? *Ans:* 22 players.
   b) How many players are in three teams? *Ans:* 33 players.
   c) How many players are in four teams? *Ans:* 44 players.

41. If Glenn read 25 really good books, 10 not so good, and 15 really awful
   ones. How many books did he read? *Ans:* 50 books.

Adding double-digit numbers ending in 0

Exercise I

- Let's count by ten up to 100: 10, 20, 30, 40, 50, 60, 70, 80, 90, 100.
- Count backwards down to 0 by ten: 100, 90, 80, 70, etc.
- If we count by ten, what number comes after 30? After 50? After 70? After 80?
- If we count by up to 100 by adding 10, what comes before 90? Before 70? Before 60? Before 30? Before 20? Before 10?

Exercise II

$10 + 10 = 20$	$10 + 40 = 50$	$50 + 40 = 90$
$20 + 10 = 30$	$30 + 30 = 60$	$40 + 40 = 80$
$30 + 10 = 40$	$10 + 50 = 60$	$40 + 30 = 70$
$20 + 20 = 40$	$20 + 50 = 70$	$40 + 50 = 90$
$40 + 10 = 50$	$60 + 10 = 70$	$50 + 50 = 100$
$50 + 10 = 60$	$10 + 70 = 80$	$10 + 20 + 30 + 40 = 100$
$10 + 30 = 40$	$20 + 60 = 80$	$30 + 30 + 30 = 90$
$10 + 40 = 50$	$10 + 10 + 20 = 40$	$50 + 10 + 10 = 70$
$20 + 30 = 50$	$10 + 20 + 30 = 60$	$20 + 20 + 20 + 20 = 80$
$10 + 10 + 10 = 30$	$20 + 20 + 20 = 60$	$20 + 20 + 20 + 20 + 20 = 100$
$30 + 20 = 50$	$10 + 80 = 90$	$30 + 20 + 20 = 70$
$20 + 40 = 60$	$20 + 70 = 90$	$40 + 20 + 20 = 80$
$10 + 50 = 60$	$30 + 50 = 80$	$50 + 20 + 20 = 90$
$20 + 40 = 60$	$10 + 90 = 100$	$40 + 20 + 20 = 80$

Exercise III

$12 + 10 = 22$	$27 + 20 = 47$	$43 + 30 = 73$	$20 + 59 = 79$
$12 + 40 = 52$	$37 + 20 = 57$	$40 + 40 = 80$	$19 + 70 = 89$
$12 + 20 = 32$	$47 + 20 = 67$	$44 + 40 = 84$	$22 + 60 = 82$
$12 + 30 = 42$	$57 + 20 = 77$	$80 + 11 = 91$	$34 + 50 = 84$
$12 + 50 = 62$	$77 + 20 = 97$	$40 + 11 = 51$	$34 + 20 = 54$
$12 + 60 = 72$	$33 + 20 = 53$	$63 + 20 = 83$	$34 + 40 = 74$
$12 + 70 = 82$	$33 + 30 = 63$	$40 + 53 = 93$	$40 + 26 = 66$
$12 + 80 = 92$	$40 + 30 = 70$	$30 + 56 = 86$	$19 + 80 = 99$

Word Problems

1. I have 10 fingers (count thumbs as fingers) and my mom has 10. How many fingers do we have together? *Ans:* 20 fingers.
    a) My dad also has 10 fingers. How many fingers do all three of us have?
       Ans: 30 fingers.

2. Tim had $20 and borrowed another $10. How much money does he have now? *Ans:* $30.

3. The Belgian Olympic team has 20 athletes and the French team has 30. How many athletes are on both teams?
    Ans: 50 athletes. Can you find Belgium and France on the map?

4. For the city marathon, Olden ran 20 miles from the start to the finish and then another 20 miles back. How many miles did Olden run?
    Ans: 40 miles.

5. Fran's aunt turned 40 today.
    a) How old she will be in 10 years? *Ans:* 50 years old.
    b) How old she will be in 20 years? *Ans:* 60 years old.
    c) How old she will be in 30 years? *Ans:* 70 years old.

6. My brother is 10 now.
    a) How old he will be in 30 years? *Ans:* 40 years old.
    b) How old he will be in 40 years? *Ans:* 50 years old.
    c) How old he will be in 90 years? *Ans:* 100 years old.

7. An ice cream store has 20 fruit flavors and 30 other flavors. How many flavors do they have? *Ans:* 50 flavors.

8. Aunt Greta's dining set has 20 spoons and 40 forks. How many spoons and forks are in the set? *Ans:* 60 spoons and forks.

9. The tallest building in our town is 20 story high. In the big town 40 miles away, the tallest building has 20 stories more than our building. How tall is the building in the next town? *Ans:* 40 stories (not miles).

10. It takes 20 nails to make a birdhouse. For a doghouse, it takes 40. How many nails will I need for both? *Ans:* 60 nails.

11. On the field trip, Curtis took 20 pictures and Don took 30. How many pictures did they both take? *Ans:* 50 pictures.

12. In one year, Leonardo drew 30 pictures and Rafael did 40. How many pictures did both draw? *Ans:* 70 pictures.

13. Yesterday, Jim read 20 pages from the book. Today, he read another 20. If he reads 20 more pages tomorrow, how many pages would it be altogether? *Ans:* 60 pages.

14. Lucien, an opera singer, has 30 fancy hats and 40 hats for every day. How many hats does he have? *Ans:* 70 hats. He has only one head, though.

15. Victor did 20 pushups in the morning and 30 pushups in the afternoon. How many pushups did he do? *Ans:* 50 pushups.

16. The farm has 20 big horses, 20 small horses and 10 ponies. How many animals does the farm have? *Ans:* 50 animals.

17. A gardener planted 10 peach trees and 60 apple trees. How many trees did she plant? *Ans:* 70 trees.

18. In Venice, on St. Mark's square, a tourist counted 40 pigeons and 20 sparrows. How many birds did he count? *Ans:* 60 birds.

19. I won 50 games in table tennis and lost 20. How many games did I play? *Ans:* 70 games.

20. A teacher graded 50 homework assignments yesterday and 50 today. How many homework assignments did she grade?
Ans: 100 assignments.

21. In the parking lot, RJ saw 20 red cars, 30 white cars and 20 green cars. How many cars of all 3 colors did he see? *Ans:* 70 cars.

22. There are 30 days in April, 30 days in June and 30 days in September. How many days are in all 3 months? *Ans:* 90 days.

23. Lora paid $10 for the shirt, $20 for the pants and $30 for the shoes. How much did she spend? *Ans:* $60.

24. Randy knows 20 words in Spanish, 20 words in French and 40 words in Japanese. How many foreign words does he know? *Ans:* 80 words.

25. Mom's phone stores 50 of her friend's numbers, 20 of her relative's numbers and 20 business numbers. How many numbers does her phone store?
Ans: 90 numbers.

26. At the Special Olympics, there were 30 runners, 20 swimmers, 10 tennis players and 10 bicycle racers. How many athletes competed at the Special Olympics?
Ans: 70 athletes.

27. In April, a mechanical shop fixed 60 trucks, 20 vans and 20 bulldozers. How many machines did the shop fix in April? *Ans:* 100 machines.

28. The city ordered 40 "STOP" signs, 30 "NO TURN" signs and 20 "NO PARKING" signs. How many street signs did the city order?
Ans: 90 signs.

29. Looking at the old pirates' map, a treasure hunter walked from the oak tree 30 steps to the west, then 30 steps to the north, then 30 more steps to the west. How many steps did he take? *Ans:* 90 steps.

30. The library bought 10 children's books, 40 chapter books and 30 text-books. How many books did they buy altogether? *Ans:* 80 books.

31. I put two 20-cent stamps, one 30-cent stamp, and one 10-cent stamp on the parcel. How much was the postage?
Ans: 80 cents. (20 + 20 + 30 + 10 = 80)

32. If a puppy was born 20 days ago, how old he will be in 30 days?
Ans: 50 days old.

33. The hole in the ground is 10 feet deep. A pole next to the hole is 20 feet tall. What is the distance between the top of the pole and bottom of the hole? *Ans:* 30 feet (you can draw a picture if necessary).

34. There are 54 white pearls and 20 black ones in the necklace. How many pearls are there in all? *Ans:* 74 pearls.

35. On a lake, Gillian caught 43 fish and Heather caught 40. How many did they catch together? *Ans:* 83 fish.

36. My cousin Igor is 12 years old.
    a) How old is he going to be in 10 years? *Ans:* 22 years old.
    b) How old is he going to be in 20 years? *Ans:* 32 years old.
    c) How old is he going to be in 50 years? *Ans:* 62 years old.

37. My uncle Nelson is 38 years old.
    a) How old is he going to be in 20 years? *Ans:* 58 years old.
    b) How old is he going to be in 30 years? *Ans:* 68 years old.
    c) How old is he going to be in 60 years? *Ans:* 98 years old.

38. Consuela has 47 stamps in her collection. She bought 30 more. How many stamps are in her collection now? *Ans:* 77 stamps.

39. Linda spent $57 in the store and Mitch spent $30. How much money did they spend together? *Ans:* $87.

40. Frank spends 27 minutes on getting dressed and 20 minutes eating breakfast. How much time does it take for both? *Ans:* 47 minutes.

41. A frog caught 58 flies and 40 mosquitoes. How many pests did the frog catch? *Ans:* 98 pests.

Lesson 31

Subtracting double-digit numbers ending in 0

Exercise I

50 - 30 = 20	40 - 20 = 20	80 - 30 = 50	90 - 50 = 40
60 - 20 = 40	40 - 10 = 30	70 - 50 = 20	90 - 70 = 20
30 - 20 = 10	70 - 40 = 30	70 - 40 = 30	80 - 40 = 40
70 - 30 = 40	90 - 70 = 20	90 - 30 = 60	60 - 30 = 30
50 - 40 = 10	80 - 60 = 20	80 - 70 = 10	40 - 20 = 20
80 - 50 = 30	60 - 50 = 10	80 - 40 = 40	30 - 20 = 10

Exercise II

90 - 20 - 30 = 40	100 - 20 = 80	100 - 80 = 20	100 - 60 - 30 = 10
70 - 30 - 30 =10	100 - 30 = 70	100 - 90 = 10	100 - 20 - 20 - 20 = 40
80 - 40 - 20 = 20	100 - 40 = 60	100 - 50 - 10 = 40	100 - 30 - 30 - 30 = 10
90 - 20 - 30 - 40 = 0	100 - 60 = 40	100 - 50 - 40 = 10	100 - 40 - 40 - 20 = 0
100 - 50 = 50	100 - 70 = 30	100 - 30 - 20 = 50	100 - 30 - 20 - 30 = 20

Exercise III

57 - 30 = 27	79 - 30 = 49	93 - 30 = 63	71 - 50 = 21
45 - 20 = 25	81 - 50 = 31	93 - 60 = 33	62 - 50 = 12
88 - 20 = 68	81 - 70 = 11	93 - 70 = 23	62 - 30 = 32
79 - 40 = 39	83 - 60 = 23	71 - 30 = 41	68 - 40 = 28
79 - 50 = 29	93 - 20 = 73	71 - 40 = 31	99 - 50 = 49

Word Problems

1. Leona had 80 tickets to the school concert. She sold 20 tickets to her neighbors. How many tickets were left? *Ans:* 60 tickets.

2. There were 40 days before vacation. After 30 days had passed, how many days were left? *Ans:* 10 days.

3. We came 60 minutes before the game and waited in line for 40 minutes. How much time is left before the game? *Ans:* 20 minutes.

4. A kennel has 70 dogs and cats. There are 30 cats. How many dogs are in the kennel? *Ans:* 40 dogs.

5.   The medicine cost $40. Tracy gave a $50 bill to the cashier. How much did she receive? *Ans:* $10.

6.   The post office received 80 packages and delivered 50 packages the same day. How many packages are left to be delivered? *Ans:* 30 packages.

7.   A grocery store had 40 paper bags and 30 plastic bags. By the end of the day they had only 10 bags left. How many bags were used?
     Ans: 60 bags (40 + 30 = 70, 70 - 10 = 60).

8.   The letter needs 60 cents worth of stamps. I attached a 40 cent stamp to the envelope. What stamp do I have to add to send the letter?
     Ans: A 20-cent stamp.

9.   There are 50 staples in the stapler and Tammy used 20. How many were left? *Ans:* 30 staples.

10. A wire is 100 inches long.
     a) How much wire does Olga have to cut off for a piece 50 inches long?
        Ans: 50 inches.
     b) How much will she cut to make a 60-inch wire? *Ans:* 40 inches.
     c) How much will she cut to make a 90-inch wire? *Ans:* 10 inches.
     d) How much will she cut to make an 80-inch wire? *Ans:* 20 inches.
     e) How much will she cut to make a 70-inch wire? *Ans:* 30 inches.

11. Out of 90 pages in the book, Kim read 20. How many pages are left?
     Ans: 70 pages.

12. Out of 70 walnuts, Mina shelled 40. How many unshelled walnuts remain? *Ans:* 30 walnuts.

13. Among 80 recruits for a police academy, there are 30 women. How many men joined the academy? *Ans:* 50 men.

14. The factory ordered 60 cases of paper. Today, it received 40 cases. How many more cases are expected? *Ans:* 20 cases.

15. A police officer wrote 80 tickets. There were 50 parking tickets and the rest were for speeding. How many speeding tickets did the officer write?
     Ans: 30 tickets.

16. Out of 100 guests who were invited to the wedding, only 80 people came. How many guests could not come? *Ans:* 20 guests.

17. Out of 90 days last fall, it rained for 30 days. On many days didn't it rain?
     Ans: 60 days.

18. Grandpa was born 60 years ago.
     a) How old was he 40 years ago? *Ans:* 20 years old.

b) How old was he 20 years ago? *Ans:* 40 years old.

c) How old was he 50 years ago? *Ans:* 10 years old.

19. A store ordered 90 boxes of cereal. There were 50 boxes of corn flakes. How many boxes were of another kind? *Ans:* 40 boxes.

20. The big dog weighs 80 pounds. The small dog weighs only 20 pounds. By how much heavier is the big dog than the small dog? *Ans:* 60 pounds.

21. Blair had $90 and gave Jess $70. How much money does Blair have now? *Ans:* $20.

22. In the building, out of 90 offices, only 60 are occupied. How many are empty? *Ans:* 30 offices.

23. A redwood tree is 100 feet tall. An oak tree is 40 feet shorter. How tall is the oak tree? *Ans:* 60 feet.

24. Garrett carries a 60 pound backpack. Colby's backpack is 20 pounds lighter. What is the weight of Colby's backpack? *Ans:* 40 pounds.

25. My dad's fishing boat is 60 feet long. My uncle's boat is 10 feet shorter than my dad's. How long is my uncle's boat? *Ans:* 50 feet.

26. In a 90 page magazine, 20 pages have ads. How many pages don't have ads? *Ans:* 70 pages.

27. A nursery had 100 rose bushes. They sold 30 and then 20 more. How many rose bushes were left? *Ans:* 50 bushes.

28. A magician learned 80 magic tricks but forgot 40. How many did he remember? *Ans:* 40 magic tricks.

29. A deli received an order for 80 sandwiches: 40 with turkey, 20 with ham, and the rest with tuna. How many tuna sandwiches were ordered? *Ans:* 20 tuna sandwiches.

30. Out of 100 nails in a box, a carpenter used 30 for his first project and 70 for his second project. How many nails were left? *Ans:* 0 nails or none.

31. From an allowance of $66, Rhea spent $20. How much does she have left? *Ans:* $46.

32. Out of 55 words, Tarzan spelled correctly 30. How many words did he spell incorrectly? *Ans:* 25 words.

33. At a kite-flying competition, only 60 kites out of 73 flew up in the air. How many didn't? *Ans:* 13 kites.

34. Hannah counted 68 jelly beans in a bag and then took out 30. How many beans did she leave in the bag? *Ans:* 38 jelly beans.

35. Out of 73 books on the library shelf, 40 were sent for rebinding. How many books stayed on the shelf? *Ans:* 33 books.

ROCHA̶̶̶ ̶̶̶ ̶̶RANCH
Dʌ̶ ̶ ̶ ̶ ̶ ̶̶

Our Products

The Reading Lesson Book

Step by step, this 444 page book introduces new letters, sounds and words to your child. The book is divided into twenty lessons. Each lesson has stories, and fun activities. Suitable for children as young as three years old.

The Reading Lesson CD-ROM

The CD-ROM makes reading come alive. Giggle Bunny, our little mascot, will delight your child while teaching the art of blending sounds and reading new words. This is an extensive CD-ROM with hundreds of games and activities. The CD-ROM closely follows the book but offers an entertaining and fun way to learn.

The StoryBook

While Reading Lesson CD-ROM concentrates on learning new sounds and words, the StoryBook helps your child with real reading. The stories start simple and become longer as your child progresses. Sweet and attractive pages can be printed to make little books.

The Writing Lesson CD-ROM

Practice, practice, practice. That's what the child needs to learn to write. The Writing Lesson program brings you a collection of never-ending supply of practice worksheets. Three different styles are included in one CD - Primary, Script and Cursive.

Big Words for Little Kids

Advanced vocabulary for elementary school children

Verbal Math Lesson series

Currently there are three books in this series. We are working on more. Copy of each book *without answers* which can be handed to the child are available at our website in eBook form.

For more information, please see our websites
www.readinglesson.com
www.mathlesson.com